Sharing the Christmas Story

15 The Chambers, Vineyard
Abingdon OX14 3FE
brf.org.uk

Bible Reading Fellowship (BRF) is a charity (233280)
and company limited by guarantee (301324),
registered in England and Wales

ISBN 978 1 80039 106 2
First published 2022
Reprinted 2022
10 9 8 7 6 5 4 3 2 1
All rights reserved

Acknowledgements
Unless otherwise stated, scripture quotations are taken from The Holy Bible, New
International Version (Anglicised edition) copyright © 1979, 1984, 2011 by Biblica.
Used by permission of Hodder & Stoughton Publishers, an Hachette UK company.
All rights reserved. 'NIV' is a registered trademark of Biblica. UK trademark number
1448790. Scripture quotations marked with the following abbreviations are taken from
the version shown. NRSV: The New Revised Standard Version of the Bible, Anglicised
Edition, copyright © 1989, 1995 by the Division of Christian Education of the National
Council of the Churches of Christ in the USA. Used by permission. All rights reserved.
ISV: The Holy Bible: International Standard Version. Release 2.0, Build 2015.02.09.
Copyright © 1995–2014 by ISV Foundation. All rights reserved internationally. Used by
permission of Davidson Press, LLC. KJV: the Authorised Version of the Bible (The King
James Bible), the rights in which are vested in the Crown, reproduced by permission of
the Crown's Patentee, Cambridge University Press.

Benediction (p. 126) © Christian Aid 2021. Used by permission.

Every effort has been made to trace and contact copyright owners for material used
in this resource. We apologise for any inadvertent omissions or errors, and would ask
those concerned to contact us so that full acknowledgement can be made in the future.

A catalogue record for this book is available from the British Library

Printed and bound by CPI Group (UK) Ltd, Croydon CR0 4YY

SHARING THE CHRISTMAS STORY

From reading to
living the gospel

Sally Welch

To Jan Fielden,
with thanks for all her support and friendship

Contents

Introduction

One hundred years ago, in 1922, at a church in south London, the Fellowship of St Matthew was begun in response to a congregation's eagerness for informed and helpful support in building a habit of daily Bible reading. In 1926, it became known as the Bible Reading Fellowship (BRF) as its influence spread and more and more church communities subscribed to the notes and prayers which were offered.

Today, BRF resources people and groups as they grow in faith, encouraging them to deepen their relationship with God and to share the good news of Jesus Christ with others.

These Advent reflections are written in response to BRF's vision of 'Sharing the Story', by looking at the events surrounding the birth of the Messiah. They will take you on a journey through familiar and unfamiliar parts of the Bible, reading and reflecting on our Christian faith.

This journey does not involve a traditional, chronological approach. Rather, each week it explores one of the themes of Advent and Christmas. Beginning with God's *promises*, shared with us by the prophets throughout the Old Testament, we see how the incarnation is the fulfilment of all those promises. The *light* of the world has descended from heaven to live among us, and we explore the nature of that light and all that it has brought to those who live in the darkness of fear, sickness or mourning. Our explorations will not take us far, however, before we engage in the *mystery* of the overshadowing of Mary by the Holy Spirit, and the wonderful complexity of Jesus Christ, fully divine and fully human. However, the *love* which surrounds us, offering us healing and comfort, support and encouragement, is made real at the moment of the birth of Jesus – someone we can trust in and depend upon when the challenges of life threaten to overwhelm us.

In Week 5, the issues which surround the nature of *peace* are engaged with, as we not only recognise the gap between the 'now' and the 'not yet' but also celebrate the gift of peace which Christ's life, death and resurrection make available to us. Finally, we look forward in *hope* to all that Christ's birth brings to humanity and the final reconciliation which will take place in heaven and on earth.

Each of these themes is explored through a daily focal point, beginning with a closer look at some of the *prophecies* given in both Old and New Testaments. While the nativity story is, obviously, the story of a birth, it is also a story of *journeys* – to and from towns and cities, friends and relatives, distant lands and hostile powers. Although the story has the birth of Christ at its centre, there are also other *babies* – both named, such as John, and unnamed, such as those slaughtered by Herod. The story is punctuated by many *signs* of change, announcements of the birth of the Messiah, and these too are explored. Thousands of *poems* and *stories* have been woven around Christ's birth, and on Fridays and Saturdays we look at biblical examples of these. Finally, at the end of each week, we look at *conversations* which take place – with friends, with relatives, with God and with our innermost hearts.

The birth of Christ is a golden point in the overarching narrative of God's relationship with his children. By looking both back and forward as we move towards this point we can truly appreciate the anticipation with which this event was greeted, the nature of its happening and the transformation which was its result. Then we can turn and share with our neighbour our joy and hope in the future of God's kingdom.

Sharing the Christmas story as an individual

Every week in Advent you will be introduced to a different component of the nativity, gradually building a picture of all that the birth of Christ means to humanity and the world. A short Bible passage is followed by a reflection, a prayer and some questions to help you reflect for yourself on the passage.

You might like to read the passage out loud, slowly and carefully, allowing time to let the words sink in, pausing at the end of each sentence. You might take one sentence or word which stands out for you and learn it by heart, holding it in your thoughts throughout the day, perhaps journalling what it has come to mean for you by the evening.

At the end of each week there is a suggestion for a creative prayer and further questions, which can be used by both groups and individuals.

Sharing the Christmas story as a group

The readings and reflections in this book have been set out so that a rhythm of daily study and prayer can be established. In this way a habit of daily encounter with God, which will build us up in our faith and encourage us on our journey, can be formed, renewed or reinforced. I have also tried to encourage the habit of theological reflection by including questions to think about at the end of each day's reflection. These questions can be used by individuals, but also as a group to reflect on the theme of the week.

The readings and reflections in this book can be used in different ways by all sorts of groups. They can form the basis for a weekly Advent group or provide topics of discussion at Advent lunches or suppers. They can be used as conversation starters for groups that already meet, such as midweek fellowship groups, Mothers' Union meetings or men's breakfasts.

If a new group is beginning and is meeting in person, it is a good idea to include refreshments with each meeting – some groups find an evening meal with discussion round the table very popular, while others feel that drinks and biscuits or cake are more appropriate. This kind of hospitality can break down barriers and introduce people to each other in a relaxed way, which in turn will lead to a livelier, more fruitful discussion.

If you are leading a group, remember that everyone will need their own copy of the book well before the beginning of Advent.

Suggestions for group meetings

The group leader may or may not also be the group host. Either or both of these roles may be fixed for the whole of Advent or rotate among the group.

If the group leader and host are different people, they should liaise beforehand to ensure arrangements are in place, the time and date are fixed and refreshments are available.

Introduction
Make sure each person has a copy of the book and that spares are available for those who do not. Introduce newcomers to the group, and make them feel welcome. Remind everyone that they do not have to contribute to the discussion if they don't want to, but that conversation will be livelier if they do!

Opening prayer
Use a prayer within the traditions of the group; this will help put people at ease, and those who are familiar with the traditions will lend confidence to those who are not. A song or hymn can be sung.

Discussion
If the group is large, split into twos or threes to discuss reactions to the week's reflections. Allow time for each person to share, if they wish. If discussion is slow to start, suggest that each person offers one word or sentence that sums up their reaction.

Forum
As one group, try to discern some themes that are common to most people. If it helps, write these down and circulate them among the group.

Reflection
Study the group questions, and spend some time in silence so that individuals can reflect on the theme personally. Come together to discuss the questions. Again, if the group is large, it is helpful to split into smaller groups.

Plenary
The leader draws together the themes arising from the discussion and sees whether they mirror those from the week's reflections. Again, these can be noted for later distribution.

Prayer
It can be helpful to begin your prayer time with silence, in order to meditate on the results of the discussion. Suggestions for creative prayer can be found at the end of every week – these can be used in a group or as an individual. This can be followed by open prayer. Be flexible, allowing time for each person to contribute if they wish.

Closing prayer

Week 1 | Thursday 1 December–Sunday 4 December

Promise

In these first few days of Advent we look at the promises of the season. Promises are powerful things – they take looking forward seriously and make claims for the future that can be depended upon. Human promises might be more fragile, but those made by God to human beings are certain – lives can be built upon the foundation of God's promises. Some of those that are explored are reminders of promises made long ago by God which have almost faded from human memory – but are still being honoured by God. Others are minted new for this season, so that we are able to join in with Mary to celebrate the imminent arrival of the Messiah as we prepare ourselves for the transformation of the world.

| Thursday 1 December

Signs

Isaiah 11:1–5

A shoot will come up from the stump of Jesse;
  from his roots a Branch will bear fruit.
The Spirit of the Lord will rest on him –
  the Spirit of wisdom and of understanding,
  the Spirit of counsel and of might,
  the Spirit of the knowledge and fear of the Lord –
and he will delight in the fear of the Lord.
He will not judge by what he sees with his eyes,
  or decide by what he hears with his ears;
but with righteousness he will judge the needy,
  with justice he will give decisions for the poor of the earth.
He will strike the earth with the rod of his mouth;
  with the breath of his lips he will slay the wicked.
Righteousness will be his belt
  and faithfulness the sash around his waist.

 Reflection

For 40 years the Assyrian armies had ravaged the lands of the people of Israel. They captured the inhabitants of the plains and hills of the fertile northern kingdoms and transported them back to their own territories as slaves. Others had their farms and settlements ransacked, their means of livelihood destroyed. It seemed as if God had forsaken his chosen people. Alone and abandoned, they were left to suffer at the hands of harsh rulers, their own kings defeated and scattered.

Living through these tragic events, surrounded by pain and suffering, it would not be surprising if the prophet Isaiah was loud in his lamentation. How hard it is to peer out into the night and see anything but darkness, devoid of hope or light! Isaiah presents us with the image of a mighty tree, grown tall and strong through years of sunlight and rain, enduring storms and gales but now defeated not by the actions of nature but by a greedy and rapacious humanity, which seeks only to exploit everything it can and destroy that which remains. Nothing is left of seasons of growth but the stump, bare and useless, a symbol of all that has been lost. All that can be done is gaze at the tree rings, tale bearers of winds and sunshine, markers of the events of many years. All that can be done is remember and grieve for lost times.

But the story is not over; the tale is not complete. As the prophet looks in mourning at the sad remains of a mighty nation, he sees signs of hope: 'A shoot will come up from the stump of Jesse' (v. 1). Barely visible among the wreckage, a sapling is slowly emerging. It is fragile and thin, a direct contrast to the mighty tree from which it comes, but still it is gaining in strength. The roots of the tree were not destroyed when it was felled; they remain deep underground, providing nutrients and support for new growth. This branch will be filled with the Spirit of God, we are promised. A new way of living and being will be demonstrated in the life of this small, humble product of a former mighty age.

For those of us who live in the northern hemisphere, the season of Advent does indeed take place in darkness. The days are short and cold. Summer is a distant memory, and spring is many months away. It can be hard to look forward in hope – easier to settle ourselves disconsolately on the tree stumps of our hopes and dreams and look back in regret at golden seasons long past.

But this is not the work of Advent; this is not the task which we are set by Isaiah as he accompanies us on our journey to the birth of the Redeemer. It is not for us to linger in a place of nostalgia and sadness. The past is not for inhabiting but learning from, not for seeking to reconstruct but for use as foundation stones for new and better.

Isaiah reminds us of the promises of God to his children that he will never forsake us. He holds out to us the hope of a Redeemer, one who will see with the eyes of God and not of a corrupt and broken humanity; one who will hear those who speak truth and not be confounded by the lies of the false. We are offered righteousness and justice, strength and support, a hope and a future.

And so we turn to embrace this season of watching and waiting, of quiet preparation. We look again at our roots and reassure ourselves of their sturdiness. We hold fast to the promises of God and wait for signs of a new beginning. We trust that beneath the cold dark soil of today there hides the green shoot of tomorrow, still tender and frail but offering new life to all who will accept it.

 ## Questions

- What are the 'stumps' of your life – the good things which perhaps happen no more, the new ventures which failed to materialise? Give them space by naming them, then put them aside in thanks for what they have brought you, while recognising that their place in your life has ended.

- What are the 'shoots' of your life – the early beginnings of adventures in mind or body? How might you nurture them?

 **Prayer**

Advent is patience. It's how God has made us a people of promise, in a world of impatience.

Stanley Hauerwas (1940–)

Lord, give me patience in times of darkness. Help me to remember that, although it seems as if nothing is happening, beneath the surface of the earth a new shoot is growing. Release me from expectation this Advent, so that I may experience this watching and waiting with my whole heart as I look for your coming. Amen

| Friday 2 December

Poems

Luke 1:46–55

And Mary said:
'My soul glorifies the Lord
and my spirit rejoices in God my Saviour,
for he has been mindful
of the humble state of his servant.
From now on all generations will call me blessed,
for the Mighty One has done great things for me –
holy is his name.
His mercy extends to those who fear him,
from generation to generation.
He has performed mighty deeds with his arm;
he has scattered those who are proud in their inmost
thoughts.
He has brought down rulers from their thrones
but has lifted up the humble.
He has filled the hungry with good things
but has sent the rich away empty.
He has helped his servant Israel,
remembering to be merciful
to Abraham and his descendants forever,
just as he promised our ancestors.'

 ## Reflection

So here they are, two ordinary women in extraordinary situations. One of them has lived a long life and a good one. She has been faithful in her religious and domestic life. But although this has brought the reward of stability and love, the satisfaction of knowing she has done her duty to God, her husband and her community, she still lacks that most precious gift of all – a child – and she suffers for this. For her and her husband, the time of hope is past and she must live with her dearest longing unfulfilled.

But then extraordinary things happen: her husband is struck dumb, and she is with child. What a swirl of disbelief, of joy, of hardly dared hoped-for happiness she must be living in! How many times a day must her feelings change – from excitement to anxiety and then once again to pure joy at her changed circumstances?

Then, in the sixth month of this emotional roller coaster, she has a visitor – her cousin Mary. Mary, another ordinary person, but young, very young. She is not yet married, but she is pregnant, and overwhelmed by this news has hurried to share it with her older, wiser cousin. An angel has visited her and told her she will be the God-bearer – and her life will never be the same again.

And as Mary hurries over the hills and plains to give and receive comfort and company, in her head is a song. It is not a song of fear or anxiety. It is not a song of self-concerned preoccupation about how her life has been changed. It is not the song of an oppressed people, suffering under the reign of their conquerors, forced to live under Roman occupation. It is not a song which will be sung to the mighty and the powerful.

Mary sings a song of praise for her creator, the one who loves her and her people so much that he has come down to live among them, to show them how to live. Mary sings a song of thanksgiving for her life and for the life of the one she carries. Mary sings a song of prophecy, looking forward to a time when wrongs will be righted, when the good will triumph, the poor will suffer no more and mercy will flow down from the hills to flood the plains with righteousness.

Prior to Mary's visit, Elizabeth had shut herself away: 'After this his wife Elizabeth became pregnant and remained in seclusion for five months. "The Lord has done this for me," she said. "In these days he has shown his favour and taken away my disgrace among the people"' (Luke 1:24–25). She recognised that God had done a wonderful thing, and perhaps she needed time to reflect on this and prepare for the birth. But Mary breaks in on her isolation, just as her song breaks into the perceived status quo of occupied Israel. Things will forever after be different. The news of God breaking into the world is broken between two women in a nondescript town in an occupied country. The established order is turned upside down.

This does not happen in one time or place. Mary speaks in the aorist tense, the past tense. She is acknowledging the action of God through the ages, the God who has been on the side of the oppressed and downtrodden since the time of their slavery in Egypt, the one who has been making and keeping promises since the time of Abraham. What has happened in the past will become the template for the future, and Mary is part of the path which leads towards the redemption of all people.

When we sing this song – whether as a frozen few gathered in the pews of a tiny rural church on a winter's evening or as hundreds of people joined together in glorious praise in a magnificent cathedral – we echo Mary's prayer of thanksgiving and rejoicing in the first stage of God's plan for his children. We celebrate all that has been achieved and look forward to all that will come. And we wait for the redemption of the world.

Questions

- Which part of Mary's song resonates with you most?

- Which part do you find most challenging?

Prayer

Heavenly Father, help me to join in with Mary's song. Give me the courage to hope in a better future and the strength to work for it. Amen

| Saturday 3 December

Stories

Psalm 105:1–11, 42–43

Give praise to the Lord, proclaim his name;
    make known among the nations what he has done.
Sing to him, sing praise to him;
    tell of all his wonderful acts.
Glory in his holy name;
    let the hearts of those who seek the Lord rejoice.
Look to the Lord and his strength;
    seek his face always.
Remember the wonders he has done,
    his miracles, and the judgements he pronounced,
you his servants, the descendants of Abraham,
    his chosen ones, the children of Jacob.
He is the Lord our God;
    his judgements are in all the earth.
He remembers his covenant forever,
    the promise he made, for a thousand generations,
the covenant he made with Abraham,
    the oath he swore to Isaac.
He confirmed it to Jacob as a decree,
    to Israel as an everlasting covenant:
'To you I will give the land of Canaan
    as the portion you will inherit'…
For he remembered his holy promise
    given to his servant Abraham.
He brought out his people with rejoicing,
    his chosen ones with shouts of joy.

 Reflection

''Tis better to have loved and lost than never to have loved at all.' This famous quote ends Tennyson's poem 'In Memoriam', written in memory of his dear friend Arthur Henry Hallam. The wisdom of the sentiment has been much debated, both in terms of failed relationships and the death of a loved one. But what about losing an entire country? Which is the least painful option – never to have had a homeland or to inhabit your homeland only briefly before it is taken from you?

How much must it have hurt the children of Israel to be in the situation they found themselves in at the time this psalm was written? The country which had been promised to them for generations, the country for which they had to endure years of exile, of wandering, of displacement before finally entering, the country which they hoped would be theirs for generations to come, has been snatched away from them, and the people of God are exiles once more.

What to do in this situation? The immediate answer is to grieve, deeply and wholeheartedly, for all that has been lost. This surely is necessary and unavoidable – any wisdom which might emerge from such a traumatic experience cannot come to light until the pain of the situation has been addressed and validated. But then what? Once the shock of invasion and exile has passed, how then to look at the years ahead?

For this psalmist the answer is simple – tell a story. More than simply *a* story – *the* story. The story of all that God has done for his people from the earliest of times, since God first spoke to Abraham those famous words of promise:

> I'm establishing my covenant between me and you, and with your descendants who come after you, generation after generation, as an eternal covenant, to be your God and your descendants' God after you. I'll give to you and to your descendants the

> land to which you have travelled – all the land of Canaan – as an
> eternal possession. I will be their God.
> GENESIS 17:7–8 (ISV)

The psalmist lists the actions of God in the lives of his children, he
reminds his listeners of the promises God has made and how these
promises have been kept. Again and again the sovereignty of God is
underlined – he is the subject of almost every verb, and the verses
resound with words of commitment and promise: covenant, oath,
promise, confirmed.

It could be argued that this reminder of all the ways in which God has
worked so steadfastly for the good of his people in the past simply
serves to accentuate the feeling that he has abandoned them to this
present situation. Where is the God of promises now? But just because
we cannot see him acting with us and for us, that doesn't mean God
is absent. God has been present in history since he first created the
world and set two human beings upon the earth to care for the land
and everything that inhabits it. Nothing takes place outside of God's
plan for creation, and everything is part of that plan – including those
who are in exile, those who have lost everything they have valued and
loved, those whose mourning is so deep and dark that it seems the
light will never reach them again. 'Remember the wonders he has
done' (v. 5). Do not despair, because he was with you, is with you still
and will be with you forever.

In fact, far from despairing in their current situations, the psalmist
encourages his listeners to rejoice, to 'glory in his holy name' (v. 3). All
must put their trust in God and have faith in his everlasting covenant
with his people. And that's not all – this covenant was made so that
God's children might 'keep his precepts and observe his laws' (v. 45).
This is not a transactional relationship; it is an invitational one. We
are being offered the opportunity to be not merely the beneficiaries
of God's plan for creation, but partakers of it as well, to be part of
God's plan.

By believing in the promises of God, by rehearsing his mighty acts of redemption to ourselves and to others, by living in observance of God's laws for humanity, we can play our part in saving the world. It is a huge task and an awe-inspiring commission, but it is one in which we will succeed by living truthfully and faithfully, believing in the truth of the promise, even when it seems as if all that we cherish has been taken from us.

 ## Questions

- Do you agree with Tennyson's view that it is 'better to have loved and lost than never to have loved at all'? In which situations might this hold true for you?

- List three examples of God acting in your life.

 ## Prayer

Sovereign God, help me to trust in your promises for your people. And, holding on to that promise, help me to play my part in its fulfilment. Amen

| Sunday 4 December

Conversations – with God

Genesis 15:1–6

> After this, the word of the Lord came to Abram in a vision:
> 'Do not be afraid, Abram.
>   I am your shield,
>   your very great reward.'
> But Abram said, 'Sovereign Lord, what can you give me since I remain childless and the one who will inherit my estate is Eliezer of Damascus?' And Abram said, 'You have given me no children; so a servant in my household will be my heir.'
>   Then the word of the Lord came to him: 'This man will not be your heir, but a son who is your own flesh and blood will be your heir.' He took him outside and said, 'Look up at the sky and count the stars – if indeed you can count them.' Then he said to him, 'So shall your offspring be.'
>   Abram believed the Lord, and he credited it to him as righteousness.

 Reflection

On 7 June 1971, the presenters of the children's television programme *Blue Peter* buried a time capsule under a silver birch tree outside the BBC Television Centre. The capsule contained some film, a photo album, some Blue Peter badges and other souvenirs, and it bore strict instructions that it was not to be opened until the year 2000. I was a young girl at the time, and I remember sitting close to our small black-and-white television and trying hard to imagine what life would be like

in the year 2000. Not in my wildest dreams could I have imagined that I would be a priest in the Church of England, working with the British Army and serving in a small town-centre parish!

We meet Abram in this reading just after he has successfully rescued his nephew Lot from Kedorlaomer and his fellow kings and pushed their armies back to Hobah, north of Damascus. He should be triumphant and excited, pleased to have won a great victory and restored his nephew to his family. Instead he appears strangely despondent. Perhaps he fears reprisals. Perhaps he can see only a future filled with war and bloodshed. Perhaps the joy of Lot's family upon his return has reminded Abram of his own childless state.

Whatever the cause, God now addresses Abram with loving and tender words. It is not the first time God has addressed Abram, reassuring and encouraging him, but it is the first time that Abram has responded. And his words are not hopeful, but despairing. God has promised Abram 'great reward', but Abram doesn't want this. What he truly wants, he believes he will never have – a son of his own and some land for his son to inherit.

'You have given me no children' (v. 3) – what a depth of sorrow and yearning is in those words. He may well that all his obedience, service and loyalty have been for nothing if he is not granted his soul's longing. Abram is as near to accusing God of heartlessness as it is possible for someone to do without actually stating it. It is a brave thing to do, to question God, and it must be an indication of Abram's desperation that he does so. Lack of an heir in the Old Testament world was a cause of shame, and it was often interpreted as a sign of God's displeasure. So Abram is questioning why God reassures with his words, but doesn't carry out his promise.

God responds graciously to Abram in this state of hopelessness. In a tender and compassionate gesture Abram is led outside and, gazing up at the infinity of the heavens, is assured of his lineage. But still, there is no evidence, no physical sign – just a promise. And here is where the hard work of faith begins, because Abram has to accept God's promise and believe in it, even though it seems impossible. He has an aged wife and no fixed abode. From where will he get either an heir or something for the heir to inherit? We who know the ending of this story – the gift of the promised land and the generations upon generations of the children of Abraham – must put ourselves in his shoes to understand the strength of Abram's faith as he makes the conscious decision to trust in God, and God 'credited it to him as righteousness' (v. 6).

We in our turn will experience the challenges of faith – the effort required to hold on to God's promises when it seems impossible that they will be redeemed. Perhaps we long for comfort and healing in times of sickness and grief, but we find none. Perhaps we hope for peace or search for love and meet only anxiety and emptiness. Then we in our turn might express our fear and hopelessness as Abram does. And it might be that in our questioning of God's promises we find our answer – perhaps it is only through articulating our anxiety, even if only to ourselves, that we will reach certainty. Then by turning to God and listening for his answer, we will hear the words of promise and be comforted.

If I had known in 1971 all that would happen to me, the love I would find, the vocation which would be opened to me and the service I could offer, it would have certainly been helpful. I might have worried less about my future in my teens and 20s, enjoyed them more and trusted God more. All I can do now is appreciate those of God's promises which have been redeemed for me and trust that those I still hope for will in their turn become reality.

Questions

- Look back to your childhood – what were your hopes for the future?

- How have the visions and dreams of your youth been realised in your life today?

- Can you see where and how God has worked with you as your life has unfolded?

 Prayer

Heavenly Father, as I look back, help me to see your marks upon my life. As I look around, help me to spot the signs of your love for me. As I look forward, help me to believe in your promises for my future. Amen

Questions for group study

- Reflecting on this week's Bible passages, which ones have engaged you most? Which have you found most challenging? Has your understanding of the promises of God changed and if so, how?

- Can you remember and share a time when God has honoured one of his promises?

- How good are you at keeping your own promises?

❋ Creative prayer

You will need a plant pot, some soil and a bulb.

It is probably a bit late to be planting bulbs in time for Christmas – but it is a good Advent activity nonetheless! As you plant, reflect that while you play your part by planting and caring for your bulb, you do not have control over how it grows. Remember Paul's words in his letter to the Corinthians when he describes spreading the gospel in gardening terms: 'I planted the seed, Apollos watered it, but God has been making it grow. So neither the one who plants nor the one who waters is anything, but only God, who makes things grow' (1 Corinthians 3:6–7). Remember the promises of God that he will always take care of us, and trust in him for your future.

Thank you, Lord, for your promises to us. Help us to nurture our faith in your promises by reading, studying and praying, so that we may grow strong in your love. Amen

Week 2 | Monday 5 December–Sunday 11 December

Light

Our oldest son has always been badly affected by the shortening days of winter. Although I would hesitate to describe it as seasonal affective disorder, there is no doubt that as the hours of daylight get fewer, his mood becomes lower. When he was a child, I would try to make sure we spent every hour we could outside. Even when it was cold and rainy, it was better for him than being inside in the warm.

Today, my son's job involves spending much time outside, and he is happy and healthy, for which I am thankful. As the season of winter draws near to the shortest day, we might feel ourselves becoming despondent because of the lack of sunshine or daylight. Then we have to remind ourselves to spend time outside if we can, dressed for the weather, but benefiting from the light.

So too our spiritual life can become weighed down by the darkness of grief, illness or simply fatigue and ennui. Then we must turn our faces towards the light, and allow the Light of the World to illuminate our hearts and souls.

| Monday 5 December

Prophecies

Isaiah 9:2–5

The people walking in darkness
    have seen a great light;
on those living in the land of deep darkness
    a light has dawned.
You have enlarged the nation
    and increased their joy;
they rejoice before you
    as people rejoice at the harvest,
as warriors rejoice
    when dividing the plunder.
For as in the day of Midian's defeat,
    you have shattered
the yoke that burdens them,
    the bar across their shoulders,
    the rod of their oppressor.
Every warrior's boot used in battle
    and every garment rolled in blood
will be destined for burning,
    will be fuel for the fire.

 Reflection

Whenever I hear the phrase 'Old Testament prophet', I get a mental image of an old man with a long, white beard and words of doom spilling from his mouth, surrounded by a largely uninterested, or perhaps even mocking, crowd. This prophecy from Isaiah goes against all these stereotypes, offering encouragement and comfort to a people sorely in need of both.

The people of Israel are in the grip of yet another war, this time affecting the northern kingdom. They are surrounded by suffering and desperate for words of hope. The certainty with which Isaiah proclaims their liberation must have filled them with joy. No longer will they be plagued by conflict; instead every sign of warfare will be demolished – even the clothing that warriors have used will be destroyed. From living in fear and shadows, God's people will be able once again to walk in the light.

The passage continues to prophesy the arrival of a child who will bring peace to the kingdoms, who will rule wisely and justly and spread harmony among his people. This was probably referring to an event within the lifetime of the prophet, but Christians see it as a prediction of the arrival of the Christ child.

This has become embedded in our understanding through the use of the first two verses in Handel's majestic *Messiah*. The words to this famous oratorio were written by an English landowner, Charles Jennens, in 1741, with Handel's accompaniment being composed just a few weeks later. Jennens was interested in Messianism, and he brings together passages from the Old and New Testament to tell a different story. First we hear Isaiah's prophecy from chapter 60: 'For behold, darkness shall cover the earth, and gross darkness the people' (see Isaiah 60:2). Then, however, hope appears in the words from this prophecy, followed by the well-known chorus 'For unto us a child is born', a soprano recitative about the shepherds and 'Glory to God in the highest' (see Luke 2:8–14). The rich darkness of the bass mimics the darkness with which the children of Israel are surrounded, followed by the vivid brightness of the chorus and the soprano, serving to emphasise the contrast between current suffering and future hopes.

First performed in Dublin in 1742, the oratorio rapidly gained in popularity and is today one of the best known choral works in western Europe. The music of Handel's *Messiah* is emotive and engaging, whatever the circumstances in which we hear it, but perhaps the best experience of all can be gained when hearing it in a large cathedral or church, near Christmas time. Then, amid the semi-darkness of the building in winter, the candles upon the altar, positioned by the choir or lining the nave provide bright haloes of light, focusing our attention, encouraging us to reflect upon the effect of Christ's birth on a sin-darkened world and a sorrow-filled people.

There will always be times in our lives when it seems that we are walking in darkness, when the way forward does not seem clear, when we feel as if our present condition of sorrow, pain or grief will last for all eternity. But the word used in Isaiah's prophecy, the Hebrew *zalmaweth*, is the same word used in Psalm 23 to describe the valley through which we walk. And in that psalm we remember the 'shadow of death' in which we walk, and that God is always with us, guiding us, accompanying us, so that we should not fear but walk in faith.

So too, when our world is dark, we can hold on to our faith in God – or even the hope of our faith in God, if we fear we have little faith left. Whatever small spark of faith is there, whatever slight hope remains after the hurt and the sadness have wiped away so much, that will shine as a light ever brightly in the darkness, as it is taken and magnified by God so that it is enough – and more than enough – to illuminate our path.

 ## Questions

- Who or what brightens your life?

- What signs of light keep you hopeful when things look dark?

 **Prayer**

God of light and love, keep the spark of faith alive in me, so that even when things seem dark, the light of your love for me will keep me from being overwhelmed. Amen

Journeys

Isaiah 2:1–5

This is what Isaiah son of Amoz saw concerning Judah
and Jerusalem:
In the last days
   the mountain of the Lord's temple will be established
      as the highest of the mountains;
   it will be exalted above the hills,
      and all nations will stream to it.
Many peoples will come and say,
   'Come, let us go up to the mountain of the Lord,
      to the temple of the God of Jacob.
   He will teach us his ways,
      so that we may walk in his paths.'
   The law will go out from Zion,
      the word of the Lord from Jerusalem.
   He will judge between the nations
      and will settle disputes for many peoples.
   They will beat their swords into ploughshares
      and their spears into pruning hooks.
   Nation will not take up sword against nation,
      nor will they train for war any more.
   Come, descendants of Jacob,
      let us walk in the light of the Lord.

 # Reflection

The Church of St Peter in Gallicantu lies on the outskirts of Jerusalem. It was built over the reputed site of the house of the high priest Caiaphas and commemorates Peter's denial of Christ before his crucifixion. In the main body of the church there is a small circular structure, like the top of a well, with a thick Perspex cover. Looking down, a deep dungeon can be seen where, it is said, Jesus spent the night he was arrested. Originally, the only way into the dungeon was to be lowered by rope through the top opening – now it is possible to descend into the darkness via steep stone steps which circle gradually lower until the ground is reached.

Whether this was the actual place of Jesus' imprisonment is largely irrelevant – it was certainly a prison, and the darkness and fear at the lowest depths is almost palpable. It takes little imagination to picture Jesus, bound and beaten, lying in the darkness, suffering, looking ahead to more suffering in obedience to the task he has undertaken of redeeming the world. It is a profoundly moving experience to reflect on the darkness Christ endured so that we could be freed to walk in the light.

What does the phrase 'walking in the light' conjure up for us? It is used in many hymns and choruses, with its image of illuminated people cheerfully strolling together, enjoying the radiance of God's love. That is certainly one part of it, and we are encouraged to give thanks for Christ's great sacrifice for us as he encountered and defeated darkness so that we could be children of the light.

But being in the light is not always easy. A fiercely lit mirror reflects not just our good points, but also our bad! All sorts of physical flaws and faults are revealed as we stand in the glare; things that perhaps we prefer to keep hidden or to soften with more sympathetic lighting. So too will walking in the light of God show up our dark places of personality and character – the things we do and say which we would rather not show to ourselves, let alone to God!

If we want to walk in the light, we must be prepared to hold up our entire souls to scrutiny, enduring the shame and regret which will be the inevitable consequence of such an action. Just as Christ must have blinked and stumbled when he was brought up out of the dungeon on the morning of his trial and crucifixion, so might we blink and stumble when we first begin to walk in the light, when we first hold up all our thoughts and deeds to the rigour of Christ's pattern for our lives. We remember that Jesus was arrested at night – truly a dark deed – but we also recall that Nicodemus came to see Jesus by night. He was motivated not by evil, but by fear, which also thrives in the darkness of ignorance and lack of faith.

Walking in the light is not always a joyful process. It can be challenging and upsetting, difficult and even dangerous as our way of life contrasts with that of those around us in ways which are uncomfortable and uneasy. We will not always appreciate the scrutiny of God's love calling us to account, preferring to hide in the shadows with Peter, denying Christ in order to keep ourselves safe. But however often we fall and fail, we are never out of reach; however carefully we hide, we can always be found. God's forgiveness will surround us and encompass us, helping us up and out, leading us on to the mountain of the Lord, continuing on our journey, learning his ways, walking in his paths – as children of the light.

 ## Questions

- What does the phrase 'walk in the light' mean to you? What might it involve?

- Are there words and actions you would rather were not exposed to the light? How might you express your regret for them?

Prayer

Heavenly Father, there are times when I have not walked in the light, when like Peter I have preferred to hide in darkness. Help me to put aside the things of the night and to journey with your people to your temple, walking in your ways. Amen

| Wednesday 7 December

Babies

Luke 1:8–17

Once when Zechariah's division was on duty and he was serving as priest before God, he was chosen by lot, according to the custom of the priesthood, to go into the temple of the Lord and burn incense. And when the time for the burning of incense came, all the assembled worshippers were praying outside.

Then an angel of the Lord appeared to him, standing at the right side of the altar of incense. When Zechariah saw him, he was startled and was gripped with fear. But the angel said to him: 'Do not be afraid, Zechariah; your prayer has been heard. Your wife Elizabeth will bear you a son, and you are to call him John. He will be a joy and delight to you, and many will rejoice because of his birth, for he will be great in the sight of the Lord. He is never to take wine or other fermented drink, and he will be filled with the Holy Spirit even before he is born. He will bring back many of the people of Israel to the Lord their God. And he will go on before the Lord, in the spirit and power of Elijah, to turn the hearts of the parents to their children and the disobedient to the wisdom of the righteous – to make ready a people prepared for the Lord.'

 Reflection

We are told that Zechariah belonged to the priestly order of Abijah. His wife was a descendant of Aaron, and her name was Elizabeth (Luke 1:5). What we are not told is that every male descendant of Aaron was a priest and could serve in the temple in Jerusalem. By the time we get to Zechariah, the number of priests had probably reached 20,000. They were divided into groups, with each group of priests serving for about two weeks in every year. The tasks of the temple were likewise divided up, with lots being cast for every role.

Twice a day, prayers and sacrifices were offered up on behalf of the Jewish people. According to the law of Moses, 'Aaron must burn fragrant incense on the altar every morning when he tends the lamps. He must burn incense again when he lights the lamps at twilight so that incense will burn regularly before the Lord for the generations to come' (Exodus 30:7–8). The privilege of offering incense at the altar of the Lord in his house might come to a priest only once in an entire lifetime.

Imagine the preparations that Zechariah would have undergone – the excitement, the nerves perhaps! In the morning he would have processed to the temple, watched by hundreds of worshippers. He would have entered the inner sanctuary with two other priests, whose task it was to prepare the incense and the altar, but they would have left, and Zechariah would be there, alone, to offer prayers for his nation.

We are not told what Zechariah prayed for. Might it have been a child? Possibly not – after all, his role was to pray not only on his own behalf but also for all Jewish people. Possibly too, after many years without a child, and being advanced in age, Zechariah might have felt that for Elizabeth to become pregnant was too unlikely a miracle even to pray for. But an angel appears, and the course of Zechariah's life is changed. The child of these two righteous people will be a 'joy and delight' to them, but he will have a greater task – that of preparing his people for the Lord.

We will explore, later this week, Zechariah's reaction to this momentous news, but one thing struck me when I studied this passage before writing about it. It is a simple thing, but the greatest wisdom usually is, isn't it? Before he could hear the angel, Zechariah had to be prepared to listen. Before he could hear the message sent from God to him, he had to be in God's house, open to God's word.

Joan of Arc was a 15th-century Frenchwoman, born into a peasant family, who claimed to have heard the voices of the archangel Michael, St Margaret and St Catherine urging her to join the fight against the English, who ruled France at that time. Supporting the uncrowned King Charles VII in his efforts in the Hundred Years War, she was captured by the English and burnt at the stake in 1431, at the age of 19. In his famous play *Saint Joan* (1923), George Bernard Shaw imagines a conversation between the Dauphin and Joan:

> **Charles:** Oh, your voices, your voices. Why don't the voices come to me? I am king, not you.

> **Joan:** They do come to you; but you do not hear them. You have not sat in the field in the evening listening for them. When the angelus rings you cross yourself and have done with it; but if you prayed from your heart, and listened to the thrilling of the bells in the air after they stop ringing, you would hear the voices as well as I do.

Sometimes we do not hear God's voice because our ears are filled with the noises of others; sometimes because our hearts are filled with worry and anxiety, pain or grief. Sometimes, however, we don't hear God's voice because we simply don't take the time to stop and listen.

 ## Questions

- How often do you stop and listen – really listen – for the voice of God? How might you make time to do so?

- When have you heard God's voice? How did it feel?

Prayer

Open my ears, Lord, to hear your voice. Open my mind to follow where you lead. Open my hands to serve you through my neighbour. Open my heart to your love. Amen

Signs

Exodus 13:17–22

When Pharaoh let the people go, God did not lead them on the road through the Philistine country, though that was shorter. For God said, 'If they face war, they might change their minds and return to Egypt.' So God led the people around by the desert road towards the Red Sea. The Israelites went up out of Egypt ready for battle.

Moses took the bones of Joseph with him because Joseph had made the Israelites swear an oath. He had said, 'God will surely come to your aid, and then you must carry my bones up with you from this place.'

After leaving Sukkoth they camped at Etham on the edge of the desert. By day the Lord went ahead of them in a pillar of cloud to guide them on their way and by night in a pillar of fire to give them light, so that they could travel by day or night. Neither the pillar of cloud by day nor the pillar of fire by night left its place in front of the people.

 ## Reflection

I have a great fondness for waymarks – those small signs nailed to trees, posts, fences and even houses which show that you are on the right route, wherever you are walking to. Many of them are beautifully designed – simple but effective – and their presence on the path can be enormously reassuring.

However, although I have a great affection for waymarks, and any reference to them brings back happy memories of pilgrimage, I must admit I don't trust them. They can be easy to miss – one person's 'obvious' can be another person's 'incredibly well hidden'. They can become covered with plants and greenery, especially if a path is not well maintained. They can become worn or discoloured – I have often been misled in France following what I believed to be white markers painted on tree trunks and fence posts only to discover that they were actually faded yellow! They can drop off or break so that the continuity is broken and the walker is left for many miles without any indication of the right direction. Worst of all, they can actively compete with each other, as has been the case in the past with the Route St Jacques de Compostelle in France, where it seems every nationality has adopted a different route and erected waymarks to correspond. So, any pilgrimage I undertake, I buy the maps and study them for hours beforehand, so that I know where I am going and what I might expect to encounter along the route. I photograph the relevant sections and keep them on my phone, checking against the guidebook and the waymarks that we all agree.

With this level of 'route anxiety', it is not surprising that it took me a long time to get used to using a satnav – placing my entire journey in the care of an electronic device, which only let me see a part of the way at a time. Worse still, if a particular road is blocked or has heavy traffic, it diverts automatically so the driver might end up in completely unfamiliar landscape, not really knowing where they are at all. All that can be done is to trust in the directions and keep going, hoping that the destination will eventually be arrived at.

I am reminded of my attitude to my satnav when I read of the journey of the children of Israel out of Egypt. What a huge amount of trust they had to place in God and in their God-appointed leader, Moses! The people had no idea where they were going, no sense of how long it would take, no knowledge of how they would find enough food or drink along the way. They stepped out in faith, trusting God to lead them safely.

And how tenderly God led them! He knew his people – knew how anxious they were, how afraid of the perils of the journey, how likely they might be to turn back and take up their old lives of slavery once more, preferring the certainty of bondage to the terror of liberation. So he didn't lead them the direct route, 'through the Philistine' country, because he was aware of their weakness and wanted to protect them from it. God took his children the long way round, to give them a chance to grow and mature, to reflect and deepen their faith. And all the time he provided them with waymarks. Not just intermittently – the occasional sign that they were headed in the right direction, a fitful gesture of reassurance that they were on the correct path. No, God gave them a cloud by day – all day, every day – and a pillar of fire by night – all night, every night. How comforting that fire must have been to the weary, frightened wanderers as they settled down in the desert darkness, gathered together for fear of scavenging animals or warlike tribes. What reassurance was offered of God's constant love and care for his flawed and fragile people as they sought the land promised to them for many generations.

God's waymarks might feel sporadic and inconstant to those of us travelling in unknown territory today, whether it is a journey of fear and loneliness because of illness or death, a journey of apprehension mixed with joy because of first-time parenthood or a new partner, location or job, or simply the daily journey of our lives as we encounter new people and situations. We might wonder where our signposts are, but they will be there. Perhaps we will see God's waymark in our Bible reading or hear his love in a conversation. Perhaps we will see it in the sunlight on a flower or hear it in the sound of birdsong. We just need to pause and look around us, and its light will brighten and warm – highlighting the path ahead so we can journey on.

Questions

- Think of some of God's waymarks that you have experienced and thank him for them.

- How might you act as a waymark for others?

Prayer

Lord God, leader of your people, help me to see the signs you have set for my journey. Brighten my path with your pillar of fire so that it might show me the way of your truth. Amen

Poems

Luke 1:67–80

His father Zechariah was filled with the Holy Spirit and
prophesied:
    'Praise be to the Lord, the God of Israel,
        because he has come to his people and redeemed them.
    He has raised up a horn of salvation for us
        in the house of his servant David
    (as he said through his holy prophets of long ago),
    salvation from our enemies
        and from the hand of all who hate us –
    to show mercy to our ancestors
        and to remember his holy covenant,
        the oath he swore to our father Abraham:
    to rescue us from the hand of our enemies,
        and to enable us to serve him without fear
        in holiness and righteousness before him all our days.
    And you, my child, will be called a prophet of the Most High;
        for you will go on before the Lord to prepare the way
            for him,
    to give his people the knowledge of salvation
        through the forgiveness of their sins,
    because of the tender mercy of our God,
        by which the rising sun will come to us from heaven
    to shine on those living in darkness
        and in the shadow of death,
    to guide our feet into the path of peace.'
And the child grew and became strong in spirit; and he lived in
the wilderness until he appeared publicly to Israel.

 # Reflection

I have had the huge privilege of watching the sun rise over the Sea of Galilee. At about 5.00 am I have quietly crept from my room, taking care not to disturb those still asleep, and tiptoed through the hall of the guest house whose gardens lead down to the shore. Perching on a large rock, I have sat in the immense darkness and listened to the sound of the waves lapping against the rocks and stones at the edge of the lake. In the distance I have heard the voices of fishermen and perhaps the rumble of traffic from a far-off road.

Then the bird song started. Aware of the sun's imminent arrival, they began their dawn chorus, welcoming the return of light and warmth. I have become aware of a gradual lightening of the skies to my left, an orange glow, whose source, still below the horizon, shines strongly, thinning the darkness. I have watched and waited until the rim of the sun has hovered above the edge of the mountains which surround the lake. It seems to pause there, almost yet not quite arrived, waiting for the right moment. Then it seems suddenly to leap up from the jagged silhouette of peaks and valleys until it hangs, round and perfect, in a sky transformed from misty grey to clear blue. The sun has risen. A new day has begun.

At breakfast I have shared my experience with my fellow pilgrims, and the following days see gradually more and more people sitting silently by the water's edge, each wrapped in their own thoughts as they wait for the dawn. Mealtimes are animated by shared photographs, sketches, even poems as the experience is impressed on people's hearts and minds.

Zechariah has lived in silence for months. Not by choice – the angel has silenced him, and we will explore this further at the end of the week. But now we are not concerned with silence, we are witnessing the breaking forth of Zechariah's voice in praise to his God as he shares with all those who will listen the fruit of his enforced reflection. From voicing his disbelief at the arrival of a child of his, he is now able to give full vent to his hopes and aspirations for his son. Every parent hopes and believes their child will accomplish much in their lives – Zechariah doesn't just hope, he knows. His son, John, will turn people's attention towards the one who will come after him, the Messiah, the Most High. He will prepare the way for the Saviour of the world – a noble task indeed.

Zechariah's song brings hope to all those whose lives are darkened by the shadows of fear and suffering, loneliness and pain. His voice rings out into the darkness, pointing out the signs from the east that a new day lies just over the horizon. It may not have arrived just yet – we live, after all, in the between times. But we know it is coming. And it is our task, along with John's, to share our knowledge with all those we meet, so that they too might join us as we watch and work and wait for the Lord's coming.

 ## Questions

- What does the thought of a new day mean for you?

- Have you ever seen the sun rise? Could you do that tomorrow, and reflect on your thoughts and feelings as you watch?

 ## Prayer

Lord God, I celebrate the arrival of this day, with my heart full of longing to follow in your footsteps. Help me to walk in your ways, rejoicing in all that the day brings. Amen

| Saturday 10 December

Stories

John 1:1–14

In the beginning was the Word, and the Word was with God, and the Word was God. He was with God in the beginning. Through him all things were made; without him nothing was made that has been made. In him was life, and that life was the light of all mankind. The light shines in the darkness, and the darkness has not overcome it.

There was a man sent from God whose name was John. He came as a witness to testify concerning that light, so that through him all might believe. He himself was not the light; he came only as a witness to the light.

The true light that gives light to everyone was coming into the world. He was in the world, and though the world was made through him, the world did not recognise him. He came to that which was his own, but his own did not receive him. Yet to all who did receive him, to those who believed in his name, he gave the right to become children of God – children born not of natural descent, nor of human decision or a husband's will, but born of God.

The Word became flesh and made his dwelling among us. We have seen his glory, the glory of the one and only Son, who came from the Father, full of grace and truth.

Reflection

In recent years, I have begun to learn passages from the Bible – those I find most helpful in challenging situations and the episodes I draw comfort or hope from. This is as a response to my growing awareness of the strength that can be drawn from recitation, using it both as a form of meditation and when written resources are not available. One of the first passages I learnt was this one, and it has remained my favourite. I recite it every morning and often during the day, and it has become a dear friend. The words are so rich and so profound, containing as they do the essence of the gospel, particularly verse 5 – 'The light shines in the darkness, and the darkness has not overcome it.'

The church I serve now is typical of many rural churches in that its congregation is an ageing one. There are young families, and they enliven the Sunday Club, engage with Messy Church and enjoy the big festivals. However, the prayer warriors, the regular attenders, the core congregation are further on in years. This used to discourage me, particularly when I took services in previous churches, where the congregation would often number only ten or twenty and everyone would be over 70.

But then I began to do some maths. If there were 15–20 congregants, at an average age of 60, that would be between 900 and 1,200 years of human experience gathered in one place. Corporately they would have experienced a great deal. As one body, they would have known the death of someone they loved and supported someone facing a life-shortening illness. As one body, they would have given birth, experienced great love and deep unhappiness, witnessed the best and the worst that human beings can be. They would have endured sickness, poverty and unemployment, but also rejoiced in marriage, personal fulfilment and lived in happiness. And Sunday by Sunday, they have gathered, and still do, bringing all those years and offering them at the altar, praising God in a building which in its turn might have been standing for hundreds of years.

The building might have been hosting such gatherings through the centuries, its walls soaked in prayers, tears and rejoicing, celebrating the existence of the one who makes it all make sense, the one whose life is light, a light for all peoples. There will have been times of great doubt during those years, doubt felt by individuals and whole communities, as sickness, failed harvests or conflict assailed them, but faith has continued; trust in the light, witnesses to the fact that the light has not been overcome by the darkness.

During the season of Advent, members of the church I used to serve fix a star to the church flagpole. Made of metal poles wrapped in fairy lights, the star cannot be seen during the day, but in the dark it shines brightly, echoing the hope of the centuries, passing on the light of that first star, announcing God's gift of mercy and love to all people.

And what can we do? We can rejoice in the light that shines in the darkness, take comfort from the fact that the darkness has not overcome it and shine as lights ourselves so that the darkness that others are experiencing doesn't overcome them.

 ## Questions

- What Bible passages do you know off by heart? What prayers do you have at the front of you mind? Should you consider expanding your 'soul's library'?

 ## Prayer

Lord of light, I thank you for church communities and all that they share. I pray your blessing on them, that they might continue to shine as lights during those times of darkness for humankind. I ask your blessing on me, that I too might shine. Amen

| Sunday 11 December

Conversations – silence

Luke 1:18–22

> Zechariah asked the angel, 'How can I be sure of this? I am an old man and my wife is well o in years.'
>
> The angel said to him, 'I am Gabriel. I stand in the presence of God, and I have been sent to speak to you and to tell you this good news. And now you will be silent and not able to speak until the day this happens, because you did not believe my words, which will come true at their appointed time.'
>
> Meanwhile, the people were waiting for Zechariah and wondering why he stayed so long in the temple. When he came out, he could not speak to them. They realised he had seen a vision in the temple, for he kept making signs to them but remained unable to speak.

 Reflection

We explored both Gabriel's announcement of and Zechariah's eventual response to the birth of his son earlier in the week, but here we are in between times. Here we share Zechariah's shock and disbelief. Here we witness Zechariah's boldness in questioning the heavenly apparition which has suddenly filled the temple sanctuary. Never in his wildest imaginings would the man have expected to encounter an angel, and he reacts in a totally understandable way – by questioning the truth of what the angel is saying in the face of the unassailable fact that he and his wife are beyond childbearing age.

When I was reflecting on this passage, I tried to think of people to whom I should have listened and whose words and advice I invariably questioned. The ones who sprang most easily to mind were my parents. How much advice are we given in our earlier years! From simple injunctions to take care when crossing the road and not to speak to strangers, we are cautioned and admonished from our youngest days, well into the years when we think we know it all. And so much of what they recommend is ignored by us in the arrogance of our youth. It is only later, when we find ourselves looking back and thinking, 'They were right after all' or repeating the same advice to our own children, that we recognise their wisdom.

I have gone back to my parents on many occasions to thank them for their advice and apologise for disregarding it, laughing at my younger, ignorant self. And my parents have laughed with me, because they did the same thing, as did their parents before them.

Gabriel, however, is not so forgiving. When he brings the news of the incarnation to Mary, he is tender and patient. He responds to her questioning with further explanation:

> 'How will this be,' Mary asked the angel, 'since I am a virgin?' The angel answered, 'The Holy Spirit will come on you, and the power of the Most High will overshadow you.'
> LUKE 1:34–35

Zechariah, however, is more firmly dealt with: 'You should have known better than to question God's messenger,' Zechariah is told in effect, and for that he is silenced.

The silence is not a punishment, however, it's more like a 'time out' – time when he can reflect on the message of the angel, absorb it and realise its world-changing significance. When his tongue is finally released, it is into an outpouring of praise, a recognition of the significance of the event and the pride of a new father in all that his son would turn out to be, as well as a realistic appreciation of the limitations of John's purpose as signpost to the Messiah, rather than a Messianic role himself.

Sometimes life-changing news needs time to be absorbed – whether it concerns a joyful event, such as a birth, or is more serious, such as illness or approaching death. A time of silence can be a perfectly acceptable way of dealing with it, allowing us space to absorb the significance of the event and decide how to feel about it. Sometimes news brings with it advice and recommendations. These too can be helpful or challenging, wise or misguided, and these too can be held in silence while we come to terms with our changed future. At the end of a time of silence and reflection, our response might indeed be praise to the God who is with us at all times and whose truths cannot be ignored.

 ## Questions

- Can you remember a time when you disregarded a piece of wisdom or a truth? What were the consequences?

- How useful is silence to you as a way of responding to news of a significant event? Could you make more use of it?

 ## Prayer

Be thou my vision, O Lord of my heart;
naught be all else to me, save that thou art.
Thou my best thought, by day or by night,
waking or sleeping, thy presence my light.
Eleanor Hull (1860–1935)

Questions for group study

- Reflecting on this week's Bible passages, which ones have engaged you most? Which have you found most challenging? Has your understanding of the metaphor of light changed? If so, how?

- How much sunlight are you getting right now? Should you be trying to find ways of accessing more?

- How much Sonlight are you enjoying at the moment? How might you spend more time with the Son?

Creative prayer

If you haven't bought an Advent candle, with the days of Advent marked down the column of the candle, you might like to do so. Alternatively, you can arrange a row of four candles, one for each Sunday of Advent. Before you read or study each day, light the candle. If you have an Advent candle, watch and pray while the flame burns down, or you can set a timer for three minutes. Focus on the flickering flame – each flame is different, depending on the candle, the flames themselves are small, yet they can illuminate the darkness; so fragile, yet with them you can light hundreds of other flames. Just like the community of Christians, we can celebrate our variety, shine in the darkness and share the light with others.

Week 3 | Monday 12 December–Sunday 18 December

Mystery

One of the most satisfying aspects of the best murder-mystery stories is the way in which all the clues to solving the puzzle are set before us in the course of the book – it is up to us to try to solve it before the author does so at the very end. When I fail to solve a whodunnit, I can feel cross with myself – annoyed that I didn't spot the clues or that I came to the wrong conclusion.

There is a temptation to try to solve the mystery of God in a similar way – looking for clues as to his nature, trying to piece together the various parts of the puzzle. This is not going to get us very far! God's mystery comes from the nature of his being, which is so much greater than we can possibly understand. It comes from our smallness of mind, our inability to comprehend the creator. We need to be reminded occasionally that not all mysteries can, or indeed should, be solved, and that the answers might lie beyond us at the moment. For now, we must trust in God's good purposes for us – and wait.

Prophecies

Ezekiel 37:1–6

> The hand of the Lord was on me, and he brought me out by the Spirit of the Lord and set me in the middle of a valley; it was full of bones. He led me to and fro among them, and I saw a great many bones on the floor of the valley, bones that were very dry. He asked me, 'Son of man, can these bones live?'
>
> I said, 'Sovereign Lord, you alone know.'
>
> Then he said to me, 'Prophesy to these bones and say to them, "Dry bones, hear the word of the Lord! This is what the Sovereign Lord says to these bones: I will make breath enter you, and you will come to life. I will attach tendons to you and make flesh come upon you and cover you with skin; I will put breath in you, and you will come to life. Then you will know that I am the Lord."'

 Reflection

In the great storm of October 1987, hurricane-force winds tore across Britain, killing 22 people, taking out power lines and felling 15 million trees. The storm was made even more memorable by the infamous words of BBC weather forecaster Michael Fish on the afternoon it struck – 'A woman rang the BBC and said she heard there was a hurricane on the way. Well, if you're watching, don't worry, there isn't!'

The morning after the storm I went for a walk to inspect the damage in my neighbourhood. As I rounded the corner into the high street,

I could see a knot of people standing just outside the churchyard. They were gazing in horror at the wreckage of a huge cedar which had been blown down in the gales. The branches, dark with needles, lay among the headstones, just missing the chancel roof, but crushing drainpipes and borders.

What made the scene so disturbing, however, were the hundreds of bones and skulls which lay scattered around the churchyard, disinterred by the upheaval of the roots. The ground had been in use as a churchyard since the 14th century, and layers of bodies had lain in peace until torn out of their resting place by the fallen tree. The exposed roots stretched some 30 feet into the air, and several skulls were suspended on these roots, having spread through eye sockets and jawbones as the tree grew. The skulls looked as if they were joining in a macabre dance as the roots waved octopus-like in the wind. Brought face to face with the reality of death, people sobbed or were silent, shocked into stillness by the grim sight before them.

This is the picture which comes into my mind when I read this passage from Ezekiel. The merry, rhythmic song about 'dem dry bones' by James Weldon Johnson completely fails to convey the horror which Ezekiel must have felt when faced with this vision of a valley full of bones. Undoubtedly carrying the scars of the war which led to the defeat of the children of exile, their capture and forced exile to Babylon, these 'very dry bones' must have brought back terrible memories.

Faced with such desecration, Ezekiel is then asked by God, 'Can these bones live?' Still reeling from the impact of so many bones, what could Ezekiel reply? The most common-sense answer would be, 'No, of course not. They are bones.' But confronted by the all-powerful God, Ezekiel must acknowledge that the ways of God are mysterious indeed, and not all those ways are open to the minds and experience of human beings. 'Sovereign God, you alone know,' responds Ezekiel, and with that he demonstrates how total is his trust in God and how aware he is of his own lack of power and understanding in the face of the mystery of the creator.

But God asks more than a simple acknowledgement of his mysterious ways – he requires active trust, complete engagement with the works of God, even though his purposes are still not revealed. Ezekiel must prophesy to the bones; promise them that God will bring them to life and that they will know he is God. What a powerful metaphor this is for those times when we experience seasons of dryness, barren of hope, surrounded, it seems, by death as far as the eye can see. This death might not be physical, but emotional, spiritual or creative – any of those aspects of ourselves which make us truly human might experience loss of 'life'. But however dead we feel, however bare of hope and life, we must continue to put our faith in the mysterious almighty, who brings to life dry bones and who will restore our hearts and souls also.

 ## Questions

- What sorts of death have you encountered? How did you feel in reaction to them?

- How might you bring hope to those walking in a valley full of bones?

 ## Prayer

Dem bones, dem bones gonna walk around
Dem bones, dem bones gonna walk around
Dem bones, dem bones gonna walk around
Now hear the word of the Lord.

James Weldon Johnson (1871–1938)

| Tuesday 13 December

Journeys

Luke 2:1–5 (ISV)

Now in those days an order was published by Caesar Augustus that the whole world should be registered. This was the first registration taken while Quirinius was governor of Syria. So all the people went to their hometowns to be registered.

Joseph, too, went up from the city of Nazareth in Galilee to Judea, to the City of David (called Bethlehem), because he was a descendant of the household and family of David. He went there to be registered with Mary, who had been promised to him in marriage and was pregnant.

 Reflection

Historical opinion is mixed about the emperor Caesar Augustus. His rule ended a long period of conflict and unrest; he brought peace not only to Rome but also to the surrounding states, while those further away benefitted from the stability rippling out from the centre. He rebuilt Rome and developed a wide and efficient road network, formalising an efficient tax regime to pay for it all. According to the Roman senator Tacitus, writing in the second century AD during the rule of Trajan and Hadrian, Augustus' achievements were many:

The empire had been fenced by the ocean or distant rivers. The legions, the provinces, the fleets, the whole administration, had been centralised. There had been law for the Roman citizen, respect for the allied communities; and the capital itself had been embellished with remarkable splendour. Very few situations had been treated by force, and then only in the interests of general tranquillity.

The Annals of Imperial Rome, 1.9

However, Tacitus was nothing if not even-handed, reporting that those who disagreed with this evaluation of the emperor claimed that Augustus was greedy for power, that the peace he won was 'peace with bloodshed', and that 'he had left small room for the worship of heaven, when he claimed to be himself adored in temples and in the image of godhead by flamens and by priests!' (*Annals*, 1.10).

It is in the context of this undoubtedly powerful ruler, with equivocal morals and a strong desire to extend the rule of Rome over as much of the world as possible, that Luke begins his story of Jesus' birth. As far away as rural Palestine, the iron grip of Rome demonstrates itself in commanding the population to relocate themselves for the purpose of a census. This census was drawn up so that taxes could be imposed upon all the nations under the rule of Rome. Much money was needed if Rome was to be rebuilt on a grander scale and her borders defended against her enemies.

So, with no regard for its impact upon the lives and fortunes of the conquered thousands, a decree was sent out. A population was ordered on the move, unaware of the purpose behind the order but forced to comply anyway. Mary and Joseph arrived at Bethlehem too late to find suitable accommodation and had to make do with what was available; their son was born in a room allocated to animals, adjacent to an inn.

What a demonstration of the huge gap between powerful and powerless! An emperor orders a census, and a pregnant woman and her husband must travel 90 hard miles to comply. So the birth of Christ underlines what sort of ruler the Messiah will be – all previous expectations will be overturned, all established principles of power toppled as the Son of God 'emptied himself, taking the form of a slave, being born in human likeness' (Philippians 2:7, NRSV). So begins the new kingdom, anticipated by Mary in her song of joy: 'He has brought down the powerful from their thrones, and lifted up the lowly' (Luke 1:52, NRSV).

This is a kingdom built not on bloodshed and slavery, but on peace and equality; not on political machinations and deceit, but on openness and hospitality; not on pride and power, but on humility and love. Even at the height of Augustus' reign, the Roman empire was being undermined by the rule of Christ. Soon, news of that rule would spread throughout the world, bringing hope to all who longed for a new way of living.

We are many centuries away from the empire of Augustus, but still wealth is power, the poor are oppressed and millions of people live in poverty and despair. We can play our part in overturning the reign of selfishness and greed by being alert to its signs among our own actions and the actions of our communities. We can help to bring near the kingdom of God by our promotion of peace, our generosity of spirit and our love for those with whom we share our lives.

 ## Questions

- Reflect on areas of inequality within your community and experience. What might be done to remove them?

- How might we undermine the concepts that might is right and that wealth is power?

Prayer

Our lives begin to end the day we become silent about things that matter.

Martin Luther King Jr. (1929–68)

Lord God, I pledge myself to work against inequality. I pray for those whose lives are determined by the actions of others in a way which does not benefit them and which they cannot understand. I thank you that the journey of Mary and Joseph, made by force, was the beginning of the journey to a new way of living for all. Amen

| Wednesday 14 December

Babies

Luke 1:26–38

In the sixth month of Elizabeth's pregnancy, God sent the angel Gabriel to Nazareth, a town in Galilee, to a virgin pledged to be married to a man named Joseph, a descendant of David. The virgin's name was Mary. The angel went to her and said, 'Greetings, you who are highly favoured! The Lord is with you.'

Mary was greatly troubled at his words and wondered what kind of greeting this might be. But the angel said to her, 'Do not be afraid, Mary; you have found favour with God. You will conceive and give birth to a son, and you are to call him Jesus. He will be great and will be called the Son of the Most High. The Lord God will give him the throne of his father David, and he will reign over Jacob's descendants forever; his kingdom will never end.'

'How will this be,' Mary asked the angel, 'since I am a virgin?'

The angel answered, 'The Holy Spirit will come on you, and the power of the Most High will overshadow you. So the holy one to be born will be called the Son of God. Even Elizabeth your relative is going to have a child in her old age, and she who was said to be unable to conceive is in her sixth month. For no word from God will ever fail.'

'I am the Lord's servant,' Mary answered. 'May your word to me be fulfilled.' Then the angel left her.

Reflection

We all know Mary. She's the one in blue in the nativity play, the one who is scolded by her young son when she is concerned for his where-abouts and the one who annoys him with her housekeeping issues at the wedding in Cana. Mary is the one who comes to fetch Jesus home. She's the obligation the crucified Lord hands on to his favoured disciple. Mary is the silent one, the passive one.

Or is she? Mary also sings a radical song when she announces Jesus' imminent arrival to her cousin Elizabeth. She ponders the visits of the shepherds and the magi. She accompanies him on his journey to the cross. And, in Luke's gospel, she is the first to view the empty tomb.

There are so many conflicting views around this woman. Is she the Theotokos, God-bearer, worthy of devotion in her own right, or is she simply the human vessel for the incarnation? What we feel about her will depend on our church upbringing, our views on gender, our rela-tionship with our own mother, our theology and even our politics. In short, we feel about Mary as we might feel about many people – that we cannot know all about her because she is a human being and as such is complicated, confusing and impossible to understand com-pletely, because only God can do that.

In this passage, we meet Mary at the moment when the whole world changes for her. Here, Mary is first made aware of the unique nature of her calling. Here, Mary responds in obedience to the God who created her and who will save humankind through her.

You are highly favoured, Gabriel tells Mary. How so? Highly favoured in that she will bear a child out of wedlock, risking shame and disgrace? Highly favoured in that she will never know the ordinary life which was her destiny before Gabriel came and changed everything? Highly favoured in that she will see her son beaten, stripped and crucified before her eyes?

Don't be afraid, Gabriel tells Mary. Don't be afraid because you will give birth to the Son of the Most High, whatever that means? Don't be afraid because you will follow your son to strange places and meet strange people? Don't be afraid because you will be faced with hostile crowds who will shout and curse? Don't be afraid because when you finally understand the truth of the resurrection, no one will believe you?

Who can blame this young girl for questioning – even when the bearer of the message is an archangel. After all, we saw Zechariah do just the same thing, and he had years of experience of life and prayer. But Gabriel is gentler with Mary – he doesn't castigate her; he merely explains to her how the miracle of the incarnation will happen.

And then we wait. We wait in silence, holding our breath, while Mary decides what to do. We wait, and the future of humankind hangs in the balance. We wait, and heaven and earth wait with us.

And finally, 'Here am I, the servant of the Lord; let it be to me according to your word' (v. 38, NRSV), says Mary. Her words will years later be echoed by her son in the garden of Gethsemane: 'not my will, but yours be done' (Luke 22:42). Two moments of supreme obedience to the will of God, forming the pattern for our lives as we too struggle first to understand, then to obey, God's plans for us.

We will not be asked to be God-bearers. We probably will not be asked to give up our lives for others. But we will be asked to be obedient, to follow The Way which Jesus first showed us – to care for the sick and the poor; to love even when it costs us and causes us pain; to 'be perfect… as your heavenly Father is perfect' (Matthew 5:48). We won't always manage this, but still we will pray for strength and courage to say, 'Not my will, but yours be done.'

Questions

- How do you view Mary?

- If Mary could have seen how her life turned out, would she still have said yes to Gabriel? Would you?

 Prayer

*Take my life and let it be
consecrated, Lord, to thee.
Take my moments and my days;
let them flow in endless praise.*

Frances R. Havergal (1836–79)

| **Thursday 15 December**

Signs

Isaiah 7:3–14 (NRSV)

Then the Lord said to Isaiah, Go out to meet Ahaz, you and your son Shear-jashub, at the end of the conduit of the upper pool on the highway to the Fuller's Field, and say to him, Take heed, be quiet, do not fear, and do not let your heart be faint because of these two smouldering stumps of firebrands, because of the fierce anger of Rezin and Aram and the son of Remaliah. Because Aram – with Ephraim and the son of Remaliah – has plotted evil against you, saying, Let us go up against Judah and cut off Jerusalem and conquer it for ourselves and make the son of Tabeel king in it; therefore thus says the Lord God:

It shall not stand,

and it shall not come to pass.

For the head of Aram is Damascus,

and the head of Damascus is Rezin.

(Within sixty-five years Ephraim will be shattered, no longer a people.)

The head of Ephraim is Samaria,

and the head of Samaria is the son of Remaliah.

If you do not stand firm in faith,

you shall not stand at all.

Again the Lord spoke to Ahaz, saying, Ask a sign of the Lord your God; let it be deep as Sheol or high as heaven. But Ahaz said, I will not ask, and I will not put the Lord to the test. Then Isaiah said: 'Hear then, O house of David! Is it too little for you to weary mortals, that you weary my God also? Therefore the Lord himself will give you a sign. Look, the young woman is with child and shall bear a son, and shall name him Immanuel.'

Reflection

The prophet Isaiah is in conversation with Ahaz. Ahaz is afraid, and rightly so, because he has heard some bad news. Judah and Israel, once one kingdom, had become separate kingdoms after Solomon's death. The kingdom of Israel, led by King Pekah, needed support from Judah against Assyria, which was fiercely ambitious for control over that part of the world. Judah, under the kingship of Ahaz, would not give the required support, so Israel has teamed up with another kingdom, Aram. Israel and Aram are en route to Judah, and trouble lies ahead.

But Isaiah has come to reassure Ahaz. He reminds the king that God is with him and that if Ahaz will only trust in God all will be well. Not only that, Isaiah bears a message from God, telling Ahaz that he can ask for any sign he likes as a further gesture of reassurance.

This Ahaz declines. Of course he is not going to ask God for a sign; that is forbidden. So far, so righteous – after all, we are told by Jesus himself that 'it is written, "Do not put the Lord your God to the test"' (Matthew 4:7). But Isaiah doesn't praise Ahaz for his restraint nor congratulate him on his faith that doesn't need to test God to be assured of his presence. Instead Isaiah roundly condemns him for trying God's patience.

Perhaps this is because Ahaz's relationship with God is a distant one, one that has lost the ability to trust. Perhaps Ahaz is so little used to asking God for his help and support that he fears he will not get a response. Perhaps the faith of Ahaz is so frail that silence would destroy it – better not to ask than to ask and be refused. We know too that Ahaz has put his faith in a worldly solution. In his fear of Israel and Aram, he has sought protection from the very state which threatens them all – Assyria:

> Ahaz sent messengers to King Tiglath-pileser of Assyria, saying,
> 'I am your servant and your son. Come up, and rescue me from
> the hand of the king of Aram and from the hand of the king of
> Israel, who are attacking me.
>
> 2 KINGS 16:7 (NRSV)

Ahaz cannot ask for a sign – he has already made the sign redundant.

But still Isaiah prophesies, in those glorious words which have brought hope through the centuries – 'He shall be called Immanuel, "God with us" (see Matthew 1:22–23). God's sign is not a fully armed warrior, ready to leap into action and lead the people of Judah in triumphant battle against their enemies. God's sign is not a wily statesmen, whose careful words will de-escalate a conflict situation. God's sign is a child, vulnerable and helpless, whose very weakness will usher in a kingdom more powerful than all the might of Assyria, Rome and every other earthly empire combined.

There are times when our relationship with God is so distant that we lose the intimacy and trust that frequent interaction bring. We cannot bring ourselves to ask for anything for fear we will be rejected – and perhaps we fear rejection most of all. There are times when our anxiety about the future is so great and our faith so frail that we put our trust in the things of the world – in wealth or power, status or even people. We try to avert a perceived disaster by our own actions, rather than trusting in God and his grace. Sometimes it will feel that even though we have put our faith in God, we have been abandoned, that although we have asked faithfully in Jesus' name, our request has not been granted. Then we need to remember that the things of the world are but 'smouldering stumps', hot but not deadly, that God's ways are not our ways, and that the way through the fear and the suffering, the pain and the grief, is to take hold of the hand of God and allow ourselves to trust in him.

Questions

- What institutions or concepts of this world do you put your trust in? Is that trust always justified?

- What sign would you ask God for?

 # Prayer

O come, O King of nations, bind
in one the hearts of all mankind.
Bid all our sad divisions cease
and be yourself our King of Peace.

Trans. J.M. Kneale (1818–66)

| Friday 16 December

Poems

1 Timothy 3:16 (NRSV)

> Without any doubt, the mystery of our religion is great:
>   He was revealed in flesh,
>   vindicated in spirit,
>   seen by angels,
>   proclaimed among Gentiles,
>   believed in throughout the world,
>   taken up in glory.

 Reflection

There is a classic pen-and-paper puzzle which still succeeds in mystifying countless people. Draw three rows of three dots so that they form a square. Then, without lifting your pen from the paper, join those nine dots with only four lines. When I first tried this, time and again I would think I had succeeded, only to realise that I had used five lines, not four.

The only way to solve the puzzle is to extend two of the lines beyond the boundaries of the dots. If the dots are numbered 1 to 9 from left to right down the page, one line begins on dot 9 and diagonally connects dots 5 and 1. The second line starts at 1 and moves through 2 and 3 to a point beyond 3 where the third line can go straight through dots 6 and 8, ending at a point vertically level with, but below, dot 7, before line four connects dots 7, 4 and 1.

Why am I telling you this? Because it is a classic example of the limitations we impose upon ourselves when faced with a problem. The only rule is that there should be four continuous lines. We invent the one about not going beyond the dots, and thus make the problem unsolvable.

'Our God is a great big God,' we teach our children to sing. So why do we consistently constrain him, ignore him and fail to believe that he is in fact more powerful than we could ever imagine? It might be because we are frightened to share with God the desires of our hearts. This could be because ultimately they are unworthy – we know that if we ask God to make us rich beyond our imagining, that probably reveals that our focus for life is not where it should be. It could be because the desires of our hearts are so dear to us that we cannot bring ourselves to share them with anyone, for fear we should be mocked. Perhaps we put God in a box because our faith is only box-sized – we are completely locked in by the rules of the world, whether they are the laws of science, the accepted definitions of success or a lack of experience of human love which makes believing in a superhuman love almost impossible.

Paul writes to Timothy to remind us of the 'mystery of godliness'. It reads like a credal statement, a song encapsulating in six lines the Christian faith – Jesus revealed; vindicated; risen in glory. But it does more than that: it brings us face to face with the sheer awesomeness of God made man, the vastness of his promises, the splendour of our redemption. When we are overwhelmed by our problems, frightened out of our faith by the smallness of our imaginations, we would do well to repeat these lines to ourselves. The mystery of our religion has been revealed in Christ – we know now how to live in this world because of his example. We know that the gap between heaven and earth has been healed by his death, that our sins no longer keep us locked away from God but that the doors to the box-prisons we have created for ourselves have been broken open so we can live in love and freedom. He is 'the Alpha and the Omega, the beginning and the end' (Revelation 21:6), and in him we place our lives.

Questions

- Do you put God in a box? What are the walls made of? How might you break them down?

- How might you help others out of their boxes?

Prayer

Of the Father's love begotten
ere the worlds began to be,
he is Alpha and Omega,
he the source, the ending he,
of the things that are, that have been,
and that future years shall see,
evermore and evermore.

Trans. J.M. Kneale (1818–66)

| Saturday 17 December

Stories

Matthew 1:18–24 (NRSV)

Now the birth of Jesus the Messiah took place in this way. When his mother Mary had been engaged to Joseph, but before they lived together, she was found to be with child from the Holy Spirit. Her husband Joseph, being a righteous man and unwilling to expose her to public disgrace, planned to dismiss her quietly. But just when he had resolved to do this, an angel of the Lord appeared to him in a dream and said, 'Joseph, son of David, do not be afraid to take Mary as your wife, for the child conceived in her is from the Holy Spirit. She will bear a son, and you are to name him Jesus, for he will save his people from their sins.' All this took place to fulfil what had been spoken by the Lord through the prophet:

'Look, the virgin shall conceive and bear a son,
    and they shall name him Emmanuel',
which means, 'God is with us.' When Joseph awoke from sleep, he did as the angel of the Lord commanded him.

 Reflection

What does it mean to be 'righteous'? The Cambridge Dictionary defines it as behaving in a 'morally correct way', but I am not sure that gives full weight to the meaning of the word. A righteous person is someone who lives by a moral code which is considered to be profound and good. There is a sense of strict adherence to the law, whether that be religious or secular, moral or legal. But there are overtones of a lack of sympathy – a righteous person may do the correct thing but maybe not the kind thing, the lawful action but maybe not the loving one. And there is always the possible addition of 'self' to the word, and a self-righteous person is not a pleasant creature. Self-righteous people believe not only that they are morally correct, but also that their behaviour is better than that of others. There is an element of censoriousness, of judgementalism, of criticism.

So perhaps we are a little put off when we read that Joseph was a 'righteous man'. Maybe this means Joseph stuck a little too closely to the rule of law at the expense of the rule of love.

Initially this seems to be the case. We first meet Joseph in Matthew's gospel just a few verses before our passage, as he is named in the glorious genealogy with which the evangelist begins the book: 'Jacob the father of Joseph the husband of Mary, of whom Jesus was born, who is called the Messiah' (Matthew 1:16). This recitation sets out the correctness of the relationships for the Son of God, going right back to Abraham and David, the great leaders of the children of Israel. Joseph has the background, and he seems to walk in his ancestors' footsteps. He is a righteous man.

But then we see the first glimmers of humanity. When Mary is 'found to be with child', Joseph is 'unwilling to expose her to public disgrace'. But is this for Mary's sake or for his own and that of his family? The public disgrace of Mary would lead inevitably to the public disgrace of Joseph and his house. Once again the 'righteous man' takes the lead – Mary will be put away quietly, sent somewhere to have her illegitimate child and live the rest of her life in shame.

And then God steps in – or rather, one of his angels. We read yesterday that Jesus was 'seen by angels' (1 Timothy 3:16). Here they are watching over him from before his birth. Joseph has it explained to him that the child of Mary is the one foretold by Isaiah, when he told the terrified Ahaz to have faith in God and in the sign God would send – Emmanuel, 'God with us'.

Joseph's life, like Mary's, is thus turned upside down. His role in the life of the Redeemer will be low key, behind the scenes, but nonetheless vital. It is Joseph who will work to support Mary and her baby; he will provide a safe, stable environment for the growing boy; he will teach Jesus about carpentry, giving him a taste of normal life before his ministry takes over.

Joseph's role is minor but vital, and as he plays his part in the salvation of the world, he stands as an example to all of us who have supporting roles in our homes, communities and churches. Nothing grand or dramatic is demanded of him, simply his presence and his obedience to the God who first announced that the child of Mary would 'save his people from their sins'. It is not an exciting task, but neither is it an easy one – and one perhaps which offers a new definition of 'righteous'.

 ## Questions

- What is your definition of 'righteous'? Does Joseph meet that definition?

- How do you see your role in the salvation of the world?

 ## Prayer

Heavenly Father, just as Joseph was content to provide loving support for Jesus as he grew, so might we offer ourselves as enablers of your kingdom, that your plan for the world might be accomplished through us. Amen

| Sunday 18 December

Conversations – with friends

Luke 1:39–45 (NRSV)

In those days Mary set out and went with haste to a Judean town in the hill country, where she entered the house of Zechariah and greeted Elizabeth. When Elizabeth heard Mary's greeting, the child leapt in her womb. And Elizabeth was filled with the Holy Spirit and exclaimed with a loud cry, 'Blessed are you among women, and blessed is the fruit of your womb. And why has this happened to me, that the mother of my Lord comes to me? For as soon as I heard the sound of your greeting, the child in my womb leapt for joy. And blessed is she who believed that there would be a fulfilment of what was spoken to her by the Lord.'

 Reflection

Elizabeth is six months pregnant with a child she never expected to have – 'Elizabeth was barren, and… getting on in years' (Luke 1:7). Having endured years of shame for her inability to produce a child, much less a son and heir who could support them in their rapidly approaching old age, Elizabeth is thrilled and delighted: 'This is what the Lord has done for me when he looked favourably on me and took away the disgrace I have endured among my people' (Luke 1:25).

But she has other problems – she, like the priests who served with Zechariah, doesn't know what happened to him when he entered the sanctuary. All she knows is that her husband could speak when he went in and had been struck dumb by the time he came out. He has been mute for six months. Did he write down all that had happened to him so that she and others could read of his marvellous encounter, or did he keep it to himself so that he could properly reflect? Perhaps Elizabeth wonders what happened in there, and how this relates to the miracle of her pregnancy. Perhaps she wonders how long Zechariah will be mute, what the birth will be like, how she will cope with a baby in her old age.

And then Elizabeth sees her young cousin Mary approaching, and she realises Mary is pregnant – and unmarried. Whatever troubles Elizabeth is facing must pale into insignificance beside hers! But the child in her womb has no such anxieties – he leaps in her womb, and Elizabeth is filled with the Holy Spirit.

Two cousins, two dear friends, meet. Both are facing challenging circumstances, but both are sure that their situations have come about because of God's actions in their lives, and they have sworn to stay faithful to him and obedient to his purposes. Elizabeth's greeting to Mary is full of joy and love, and Mary's response is that wonderful poem of faith in a new world. In the coming months the women will keep each other company, and their sons will journey together to transform the world.

True friends are rare and precious. Friends who can share their experiences of God perhaps even more so. I first met Julie when my second child was three months old. Her daughter was the same age and we met in the creche of a women's prayer group. Our friendship developed – we babysat each other's children even as our families increased; we started a 'pram service' together to teach our children and others the songs and stories of the Christian faith; we competed as to whose child behaved the worst in Sunday school (about equal, actually). We trained for ministry together and were ordained a year apart. Julie's ministry took her to Hereford, mine to Berkshire, then Oxfordshire, but we keep in touch, sharing (and occasionally puzzling over) what God is doing in our lives, what we are doing in our churches and how we can continue to thrive in all areas of our lives. I thank God for Julie.

Those of you who have a friend with whom you can talk about faith as well as other matters are blessed indeed. Not every friend needs to be a live human being, however. We can take comfort and draw support from writers, musicians and artists, alive or dead, who share our faith, deepening it and challenging it through their words or pictures. And, of course, our heart's companion is one who is with us always, journeying alongside us, offering constant, unconditional love and showing us the way to eternal life.

 ## Questions

- Think of five 'friends' whose conversation, art, writing or music has helped you through the years.

- Engage with them this week. And, if you can, thank them for their ministry to you.

 ## Prayer

What a friend we have in Jesus,
all our sins and griefs to bear!
What a privilege to carry
everything to God in prayer!
Joseph Scriven (1819–66)

Questions for group study

- Reflecting on this week's Bible passages, which ones have engaged you most? Which have you found most challenging? Has your appreciation of the mystery of God changed and if so, how?

- Are you engaged by or annoyed with 'the mystery of God'?

Creative prayer

The weeks leading up to Christmas can be incredibly busy, leaving us little time to consider the amazing nature of the gift that was given to us so long ago and is given to us afresh each day. Try to find some space this week simply to sit and breathe, making your breath your prayer. Find somewhere comfortable to sit. Closing your eyes, concentrate on your breathing, becoming aware of it entering and leaving your body, filling your lungs, giving your body the air it needs. Focus on this breath without worrying too much if you become distracted – just bring your attention gently back to your breathing. As you breathe, you might like to say the word YHWH – the name of God. Let your breath become your prayer as you reflect on the mystery of God and the gift of the incarnation.

> 'This is my name forever,
>   the name you shall call me
>   from generation to generation.'
> EXODUS 3:15

Week 4 | Monday 19 December–Sunday 25 December

Love

Some years ago, a mother confided to me that she was too frightened to have a second child, even though her partner longed for one. I asked her what she was afraid of. 'I love my daughter so much,' she replied. 'More than I have ever loved anyone or anything. I am frightened that I won't love the next child as much because I will have run out of love. How will it be possible to love two people as much as I love this one?'

Fortunately I was able to reassure her that I believed that such is the wonderful nature of love that it can expand to meet the demands put upon it, and that I was sure she had enough love for another baby – and to spare. A year later, when I baptised her son, I asked her if she remembered our conversation. 'Yes,' she replied. 'Of course, you were right – I just had to believe in love.'

Not everyone finds love easy – either for themselves or for others. But God has no such problem – his love stretches throughout the universe and focuses right down to each one of us. Nothing and no one is beyond his love, which is demonstrated by his willingness to share our lives on earth as one among us.

| **Monday 19 December**

Prophecies

Isaiah 61:1–4 (NRSV)

The spirit of the Lord God is upon me,
    because the Lord has anointed me;
he has sent me to bring good news to the oppressed,
    to bind up the broken-hearted,
to proclaim liberty to the captives,
    and release to the prisoners;
to proclaim the year of the Lord's favour,
    and the day of vengeance of our God;
    to comfort all who mourn;
to provide for those who mourn in Zion –
    to give them a garland instead of ashes,
the oil of gladness instead of mourning,
    the mantle of praise instead of a faint spirit.
They will be called oaks of righteousness,
    the planting of the Lord, to display his glory.
They shall build up the ancient ruins,
    they shall raise up the former devastations;
they shall repair the ruined cities,
    the devastations of many generations.

 Reflection

When our older son was twelve years old, I moved posts to a multi-parish rural benefice. The local town was a 20-minute drive away, and in those days there was only one bus there and back each day. Simon depended on me to drive him to and from school, to and from his friends' houses – to and from everywhere, in fact. The village where we lived was very nice, but very small. Simon longed for some independence – and also some anonymity, as the burden of being 'the vicar's son' can be a significant one. We saved hard and promised him a moped for his 16th birthday so that he could travel freely, and he looked forward to this greatly. Counting down the weeks, then the days, until his birthday, it felt more like being with a child of six than a 16-year-old.

Being of an anxious disposition, I worried about this, fearing that the reality would not live up to the anticipation and Simon would be disappointed with his small, underpowered, second-hand vehicle. But when the day finally arrived and Simon (CBT test duly passed) set off to travel the highways and byways of West Oxfordshire, his face was wreathed in smiles. After about a month, when the newness had worn off, I asked him whether he still felt the same about his bike. 'It's the best thing ever,' he said happily, and set off again.

Unlike my son's experience, there is often a huge gap between expectation and reality. Having looked forward to an event for a long time, we might feel decidedly underwhelmed when the day at last arrives, disappointed that what had held sway in our imaginations for so long did not live up to the experience. This appears to the be case for the Israelites in this passage. The tone seems familiar to us as we hear once again that the children of Israel are 'mourning', that they have a 'faint spirit'. We picture them once more sitting beside the waters of Babylon, weeping in exile for their lost homes. But this is not so – this passage was written after King Cyrus had defeated the Babylonians and decreed that the Israelites could return home and rebuild their city and their temple. They should be rejoicing, but they are not.

Might this be because the longed-for reality turned out to be harder than they thought? Might it be that despite their best efforts, they haven't succeeded in rebuilding better than before but are in fact struggling to rebuild at all, not to speak of the economic inequalities in the city or the conflict caused by different religious and political parties. So much was hoped for, and it was so much harder than they hoped!

So Isaiah addresses them boldly and energetically. He will bring rejoicing and gladness, comfort and praise. He will energise the weary children of Israel so that they can 'raise up the former devastations'. He will proclaim the year of the Lord's favour – that is, the jubilee year, the one year in every 50 when a debt amnesty is declared and everyone is free to begin again, captives are set free and prisoners released. Isaiah promises a time of abundance and growth, of peace and celebration. And in this promise lies its fulfilment, as the Israelites are re-energised and filled with hope once more.

Thus can encouraging words lift the hearts of tired people. Thus can words of love and support provide comfort to those who mourn. Thus can putting our trust and expectation in Jesus Christ bring about an eternal 'jubilee year', in which our hopes will never be disappointed, as it will be beyond our wildest dreams.

 ## Questions

- What are your hopes for your future? What are your hopes for your church community? How might you encourage others to have hope too?

 ## Prayers

'Today this scripture has been fulfilled in your hearing.'
LUKE 4:21 (NRSV)

Lord Jesus Christ, give me the words to preach good news, the wisdom to bring comfort and the love to provide hope in your name. Amen

Journeys

Luke 2:8–20 (NRSV)

In that region there were shepherds living in the fields, keeping watch over their flock by night. Then an angel of the Lord stood before them, and the glory of the Lord shone around them, and they were terrified. But the angel said to them, 'Do not be afraid; for see – I am bringing you good news of great joy for all the people: to you is born this day in the city of David a Saviour, who is the Messiah, the Lord. This will be a sign for you: you will find a child wrapped in bands of cloth and lying in a manger.' And suddenly there was with the angel a multitude of the heavenly host, praising God and saying,

'Glory to God in the highest heaven,
and on earth peace among those whom he favours!'

When the angels had left them and gone into heaven, the shepherds said to one another, 'Let us go now to Bethlehem and see this thing that has taken place, which the Lord has made known to us.' So they went with haste and found Mary and Joseph, and the child lying in the manger. When they saw this, they made known what had been told them about this child; and all who heard it were amazed at what the shepherds told them. But Mary treasured all these words and pondered them in her heart. The shepherds returned, glorifying and praising God for all they had heard and seen, as it had been told them.

Reflection

Once upon a time – a long time ago now – two girls answered an advertisement in their local newspaper for help wanted on a sheep farm in Devon. I am not sure which of them persuaded the other that spending time in the middle of nowhere with a load of sheep was a good idea. Each of them frequently blamed the other in the months to come. Neither of the girls came from a farming background or had any experience with livestock, but it turned out they were the only ones who answered the advertisement. So after a five-minute phone interview, they were hired and took the train to Barnstaple the following weekend.

The weeks that followed were among the hardest the girls had ever experienced. Both were headed for university, one to read classics, the other English, so they had spent the previous years reading and writing, skipping physical education lessons so that they could study rather than run around a wet sports pitch. They were, consequently, completely unprepared for the twelve-hour days spent outside in all sorts of weather, carrying bags of feed and bales of hay, herding, assisting at births, docking tails – all the tasks of a 1,000-strong flock at lambing time. Meals were mostly taken in silence, due to fatigue and uncertain temper. The girls were informed that they had been recruited from Berkshire because the farmer became so ill-tempered towards the farmhands during the season that if he employed local children he would have alienated his neighbours.

Life was reduced to work, food and sleep – and not enough of the last two. There were joyful moments – watching a lamb take its first faltering steps towards its mother; seeing the sun rise over green fields having been awake all night; walking to work through meadows rich with grass – and times when it seemed as if a particular field was the best place to be in all the world. These went some way to compensate for the sheer challenge of it all. But all the same, there was rejoicing when the season ended and a return home beckoned.

We survived, but every time I read this passage I remember the long days, the broken nights, the lack of company and the narrowness of vision that the work of shepherding involves. I found restoration in hot baths, plentiful meals and clean laundry; the shepherds of Jesus' time would not have experienced such blessings. Living on the open hills, constantly aware of the dangers facing their livestock, this group of people weren't even respected by their fellow countrymen but were instead counted as 'unclean', since their occupation prevented them from following many of the rules set down in the Torah. But it is to these people that the angels bring their news of the birth of the Messiah; to these that the message of the Saviour is carried; to these the privilege of being the first to hear the heavenly throng sing out the redemption of humankind.

And they respond! What a journey that must have been – in the dead of night, hurrying down the hills, doubtless herding their sheep before them, because who would leave one's entire livelihood on the mountain to be preyed upon? How would they have known in which stable to find the child, in which manger he would be lying? Did they run through the town, opening barn doors and disturbing cattle and people alike? How brave of them – to risk abuse and anger in order to follow the angels' command. And then to arrive, and enter the stable, and share with Mary all that had happened to them.

As usual, an encounter with Christ, young as he is, transforms their lives. Returning to their pastures they are filled with joy, turned into evangelists as they spread the news of the birth to everyone they meet, rejoicing in the fact that it was they – the lowly, the poor, the ignored – who were chosen to bring 'tidings of great joy' to the world.

Questions

- Who in our world today would be entrusted with the message of the angels, and why?

- Have you ever delivered a message which was given to you by God?

 ## Prayer

Heavenly Father, let me never forget that your gospel is for all people. Amen

Babies

Luke 2:7 (NRSV)

> And she gave birth to her firstborn son and wrapped him in bands of cloth, and laid him in a manger, because there was no place for them in the inn.

 Reflection

It's the little things that matter most, isn't it? Those tiny gestures of affection and love that don't mean much individually, but added together indicate that a person really cares and has spent time thinking about you. For me, it's the friend who sends me a link to an auction that has jam spoons (you have to love a jam spoon); the daughter who sees when my favourite chocolate is on sale and buys me a bar; the wonderful member of my church community who makes and freezes us a meal at Christmas and Easter, for those days when too much is happening for cooking to take place. I hope there are people in your life who do similar things for you – more importantly, I hope and pray that there are people in your life for whom you are able to show you care, whether through a thoughtful gesture, a helping hand or just a listening ear.

A baby is a tiny thing, but also a very, very big 'thing'. And this baby is the biggest 'thing' it is possible to be – a world-changing, life-transforming, redemption-bringing 'thing'. And yet his birth in Luke's gospel is limited to one sentence. First there was no Redeemer, then there was. Matthew tells it in the same brief way. After wading through the genealogy of Jesus, Matthew describes his birth in a single phrase: '[Joseph] had no marital relations with [Mary] until she had borne a son; and he named him Jesus' (Matthew 1:25). Jesus' birth isn't even mentioned in Mark, who begins with Jesus' baptism. And John, who hits it right on the head with the importance of the event – 'He was in the world, and the world came into being through him; yet the world did not know him' (John 1:10) – likewise omits the detail of the birth.

It can be the same in our lives too. Sometimes the most significant events or relationships begin so quietly we are not aware of their impact until we look back much later and see how they have shaped the entire pattern of our lives. This might happen with our faith as well – we might be the person who has a dramatic conversion, changing from unbelief to certainty in one minute, or we might be the person who has known about Jesus all their lives but not accepted him as Redeemer until much studying, thinking and reflecting has taken place. Or we might have begun going to church for the company, and continued for the worship as the nature of God is gradually revealed to us. Then, gradually, our faith deepens and grows as we pray and read. In just such a way, the ministry of Jesus began small, with the changing of water to wine at a wedding, then became more and more noticeable as people were healed, lives were changed and communities were transformed.

Love can be a grand, passionate, operatic maelstrom of feelings and emotions, which seizes a person and holds them captive. Or it can be the daily interchange of small gestures of affection and support, which smooth relationships and make the challenges of our daily lives more bearable. It can be between two people, a family, a group, a community. It can last forever or for just a brief while. But it all begins here, with the arrival of a baby, placed in a manger, with a mission to save the world.

Questions

- Mother Teresa is thought to have said, 'We can do no great things, only small things with great love.' What small thing are you going to do with great love today?

- How might you widen the circle of people you love?

Prayer

How silently, how silently,
the wondrous gift is given;
so God imparts to human hearts
the blessings of his heaven.
Phillips Brooks (1835–93)

| Thursday 22 December

Signs

Matthew 2:1–9 (NRSV)

In the time of King Herod, after Jesus was born in Bethlehem of Judea, wise men from the East came to Jerusalem, asking, 'Where is the child who has been born king of the Jews? For we observed his star at its rising, and have come to pay him homage.' When King Herod heard this, he was frightened, and all Jerusalem with him; and calling together all the chief priests and scribes of the people, he inquired of them where the Messiah was to be born. They told him, 'In Bethlehem of Judea; for so it has been written by the prophet:

"And you, Bethlehem, in the land of Judah,
    are by no means least among the rulers of Judah;
for from you shall come a ruler
    who is to shepherd my people Israel."'

Then Herod secretly called for the wise men and learned from them the exact time when the star had appeared. Then he sent them to Bethlehem, saying, 'Go and search diligently for the child; and when you have found him, bring me word so that I may also go and pay him homage.' When they had heard the king, they set out; and there, ahead of them, went the star that they had seen at its rising, until it stopped over the place where the child was.

✿ Reflection

I recently saw in the newspaper a family portrait of the Queen and her great-grandchildren. There were lots of them, and I didn't really take much notice, until my eye was caught by George. Son of Prince William, grandson of Prince Charles, George is the future king of England. Standing there in his shorts, with blond hair and a big grin, he looked like any other small boy. But the weight of the crown lies in wait for him. He will face many challenges, and there will be great expectations put upon him. When we pray as a church community for the monarch, it is because they have a burden which must at times be heavy indeed.

Jesus is still an infant, but the storm clouds are already gathering over his head. The magi have put all their faith and hope in a magnificent sign – a new star – which they believe will lead them to the birthplace of the Messiah. They have travelled far, facing all sorts of challenges and overcoming innumerable difficulties and dangers. T.S. Eliot in his poem 'Journey of the Magi' imagines the voices in their heads telling them that it is all folly. But still they continued. They must have had to be brave, sensible, clever and faithful in order to keep on with their task. But all this seems to have failed them on arrival in Jerusalem, where they make no bones about asking where they can find the 'child who has been born king of the Jews'.

This seems to be an extremely foolhardy thing to ask of the ruler of a captive state, and it provokes a natural response – fear. King Herod was frightened, 'and all Jerusalem with him'. Rightly so, as a leader of a defeated people could rouse an army and overthrow the current ruler. All those with a vested interest in the status quo would now be not only alerted to, but ranged against the future king, determined that he should not fulfil his destiny.

The action of the magi has begun the opposition to Christ's rule. They are not to blame, however. We cannot always control what happens to us, but we can decide how we will react. Our response to a perceived danger can be aggressive, fearful or defensive, or it can be alert but controlled, waiting to see what might unfold and how a situation will develop. Herod is a frightened man, and he lashes out against all possibilities of rebellion in a savage and widespread action of brutality.

But we are looking ahead of ourselves – the clouds are visible, but they are still in the distance, barely perceptible on the horizon. In the meantime, the magi follow the star as they have done for many weeks now. It will not stop over a palace or the house of a wealthy man. Instead the magi will find the child in a humble shelter, watched over by a carpenter and his young wife. This will surely challenge their conception of a suitable birthplace for a ruler. Perhaps here their faith is truly tried as they struggle to overcome instinctive expectations and accept reality. That they do is evidenced in their worship and their gifts – more signs of a future both glorious and fraught with danger.

 ## Questions

- Read 'Journey of the Magi' by T.S. Eliot, which can be easily found online or in libraries. What do you think of the poem? Would you agree with the poet's use of the word 'satisfactory'?

 ## Prayer

Using the poem to help you, imagine what the journey would have been like for the magi – the people they would have met; the challenges and difficulties to be overcome. Give thanks for all who make hard journeys in order to bring the gospel to people who would otherwise not have the opportunity of hearing it.

| Friday 23 December

Poems

Micah 7:1–2, 7–8, 18–19 (NRSV)

Woe is me! For I have become like one who,
    after the summer fruit has been gathered,
    after the vintage has been gleaned,
finds no cluster to eat;
    there is no first-ripe fig for which I hunger.
The faithful have disappeared from the land,
    and there is no one left who is upright;
they all lie in wait for blood,
    and they hunt each other with nets…
But as for me, I will look to the Lord,
    I wait for the God of my salvation;
    my God will hear me.
Do not rejoice over me, O my enemy;
    when I fall, I shall rise;
when I sit in darkness,
    the Lord will be a light to me…
Who is a God like you, pardoning iniquity
    and passing over the transgression
    of the remnant of your possession?
He does not retain his anger forever,
    because he delights in showing clemency.
He will again have compassion upon us;
    he will tread our iniquities under foot.
You will cast all our sins
    into the depths of the sea.

Reflection

There is a growing tradition in English churches to hold a particular type of service on or around 21 December – a Blue Christmas service. This is an occasion set aside for honouring all those for whom Christmas is not an unmitigated time of celebration and rejoicing, but is instead challenging or even deeply distressing. The service is held for those for whom the last year has been difficult. It is a time for remembering those who have died, and praying for those with whom we will not be able to gather and celebrate due to the separation of death, illness or simply distance. It is a time for looking back at Christmases past and reflecting on them, for good memories of families and friends, of meals and parties, of laughter and love. It is also a time for those for whom Christmas has been marked by conflict or violence, by separation or loss.

Not for nothing is this service held near the shortest day of the year – the day when the sun is hidden from us for the longest time, when the weather is unwelcoming and when the new growth of spring seems so far away. Not for nothing is this service held near the feast of St Thomas, that apostle who struggled with his faith and needed to see the risen Jesus in person before he would believe, not able to make do simply with the witness of others but having to witness for himself the wonder of the resurrection.

Even those of us who have not had our anticipation of Christmas marred by bitter thoughts and memories would do well to pause for a while and pray, standing alongside those who grieve, holding a space for emotions which are not completely positive, offering the suffering of the world before the cross.

This passage from Micah gives voice to the feelings of all those who are oppressed by darkness at this time in their lives. 'Woe is me!' he calls, allowing us to join him and express our sorrow, our fears, the damage of past times and our anxiety about future events. We have permission to mourn those who have died, to look back to happy times and feel their loss, and to recall past conversations or disputes and feel regret.

But we should not stay in that place of sadness, for our God is one who has conquered the darkness, who leads his children into the light, who defeats hatred with love, evil with goodness, lies with truth. Micah rouses himself from despair as he remembers who walks by his side, who leads the way, who governs the destination. 'Don't gloat,' he threatens his enemies, 'because I won't stay down forever.'

Although it can seem as if the darkness has won and that good times are gone forever, there is hope. The prophet encourages us to look back on the events of our lives and see the good that has happened; to remember the joyous occasions rather than linger on the sad ones; and to have faith in God's promises which have always proved true, rather than to join Thomas in doubting the good news of the resurrection, that event which defeated death once and for all, thoroughly and completely.

Although we pause for Blue Christmas, to pray, reflect and remember, we should not remain in sorrow, but have faith in our Redeemer and prepare to celebrate the birth of our Saviour, saying with Micah: 'When I fall, I shall rise; when I sit in darkness, the Lord will be a light to me.'

 Questions

- What are your feelings about Christmas? How mixed are they?

- What challenges does the Christmas season bring you? How can you keep hopeful and bring hope to others?

Prayer

I believe in the sun even when it is not shining
And I believe in love, even when there's no one there.
And I believe in God, even when he is silent.
Written in Germany during World War II

Heavenly Father, help me to believe in the light of your love, even
when I feel cold and dark. Help me to look back on bright times
and to look forward with hope. Amen

| Saturday 24 December

Stories

Luke 2:25–32 (NRSV)

Now there was a man in Jerusalem whose name was Simeon; this man was righteous and devout, looking forward to the consolation of Israel, and the Holy Spirit rested on him. It had been revealed to him by the Holy Spirit that he would not see death before he had seen the Lord's Messiah. Guided by the Spirit, Simeon came into the temple; and when the parents brought in the child Jesus, to do for him what was customary under the law, Simeon took him in his arms and praised God, saying,

'Master, now you are dismissing your servant in peace,
according to your word;
for my eyes have seen your salvation,
which you have prepared in the presence of all peoples,
a light for revelation to the Gentiles
and for glory to your people Israel.'

 Reflection

As a parish priest, I have always dreaded January. First, there is the languor following a very energetic December, when it seems as if the entire population of the parish passes through the church doors to sing carols and eat mince pies. This is a wonderful and joyous thing, but very tiring, and January usually sees a sharp dip in church attendance as everyone recovers from the festivities. Then, there is the fact that almost immediately I have to turn my attention to the season of Lent, which can be tremendously fruitful but also quite challenging. This combines with the short, dark days, often filled with terrible weather which do little to lighten spirits.

Worst of all, however, is the number of deaths which occur in January, as some of our oldest and most faithful community members leave this earth to travel onwards. I suppose the scientific explanation is that our immune systems are challenged by the new bugs we have picked up through gatherings and events over Christmas, but I can't help feeling that a lot of people hang on to life during December, so that they can see their loved ones, friends and relatives for one last time. In January, with visits made, conversations over and celebrations completed, the imperative for staying alive is somehow weakened and death becomes something to be accepted as the next step rather than postponed until tasks here are completed.

It is this sense of holding on until the task is done which is so apparent in these beautiful, moving words of Simeon. He is described as having the Holy Spirit resting on him – that part of the Trinity who inhabits our beings, prompting us, calling us, guiding us towards a deeper relationship with God. Simeon is clearly sensitive to God's purposes for him, but it must have been so unsettling to know that his task was to wait for the Lord's Messiah, without having been given any further instructions!

What a challenge – to be told to wait for someone without being told what they look like, how they will appear or when they will turn up. What patience must Simeon have exercised as he prayed day after day in the temple, hoping that this would be the day when he could finally carry out God's will and be released into death. The passage doesn't mention the aches and pains which an old man would carry, nor the fortitude with which he bore them, but time must have hung heavily on his hands some days, as he despaired of ever seeing the Messiah.

And then an ordinary couple appear, like so many other couples who enter the temple with their newborn, ready to dedicate it to God and his service. How in tune must Simeon have been with God, that he could recognise the Messiah in this helpless infant. But recognise him he does, and Simeon, filled no doubt with a mixture of joy and relief, takes the baby in his arms and sings out a hymn of praise and celebration. The days of waiting are over; Simeon has had the huge privilege of holding in his arms the Saviour of the world, and now, task completed, he can go to his rest, satisfied that his purpose on earth has been fulfilled.

I wonder if the challenge in this passage is how we should live our lives so that we come to the end with the same amount of satisfaction and joy? What are the primary purposes for which we have been born and raised, and how can we carry them out? This is a huge piece of emotional and spiritual work, establishing just what we are here for and what God has called us to.

On this, the eve of the celebration of the birth of the Messiah, we must surely make space for this essential task. Just as those souls who leave this earth in the early months of the year, content with time spent with loved ones, gestures of love for others and celebration of all that brings hope to the people who surround them, so will we undoubtedly discover that loving service is at the heart of what we are called to do. We may not discover a single purpose, and even if we do, it may not be as clearly defined as that of Simeon, but if we take the time to pray and to listen to the answer, to study the Bible and other sources of wisdom, we may begin to discern how we can best advance God's kingdom in a way which brings hope and life to others and joy and fulfilment to ourselves.

Questions

- If you discovered that you only had one day to live, what would you do?

- If that day was a month or a year, how might you reorder your priorities?

- Should now be the time to carry out this reordering anyway since the future is known only to God?

 ## Prayer

Heavenly Father, my time is in your hands. Help me to make good use of the time I have left to love and serve you better, and to love and serve my neighbour with all that I can give. Amen

Conversations – with ourselves

Luke 2:19 (NRSV)

> But Mary treasured all these words and pondered them in her heart.

 ## Reflection

If we are not careful, the run up to Christmas can make us feel like an overactive hamster on an exercise wheel. We rush here and there, making lists, shopping for gifts, attending events – all perfectly acceptable activities and part and parcel of what Christmas is about. However, when they are *all* that Christmas is about, we need to be concerned.

Every morning, I go to one of the churches which are my responsibility and pray. For some years I have followed the pattern of morning prayer in the Church of England Common Worship service book. This has a set structure of prayers, canticles and daily readings, with some space for individual intercessions. This has served me very well over time, providing a bedrock for my spirituality and a good start to the beginning of my day.

However, during last Advent I discovered that the busyness and activity of Christmas had overwhelmed even morning prayer. Instead of focusing on the canticles and the liturgy I was simply paying them lip service while my mind raced on, thinking of all the things I had to do that day and wondering anxiously how I was going to fit it all in and what would happen if I left anything out. My mind was in a constant whirl, and I no longer felt as deeply connected to God as I had previously. Part of this, I reasoned, was simply the effect of the season upon the vicar of a lively and active parish who thoroughly entered the spirit of Christmas – with a Christmas tree festival, advent evensong, carol services and much else. However, I also had to admit that I was not providing enough space for me to 'ponder' – to reflect, to hear God's word and to pray.

So during Advent, instead of trying to do more, read more and pray 'harder', I simplify my daily prayer routine. I light an Advent candle – one of those with numbers down its length – and while the day's wax burns through I allow the light of Christ to fill my mind with an awareness of his presence. It is a time of stillness and quiet before the activity of the day.

One of the most powerful sentences for me in the whole Christmas narrative describes Mary's actions. Surrounded by the chaos of giving birth in unfamiliar surroundings, of visitations by angels, shepherds and wise men, of life-threatening situations followed by desperate flight, Mary and Joseph remain obedient to their faith, finding time to present their firstborn at the temple and hearing the words of the prophet regarding their son. All this activity, haste, bustle – and in the midst is Mary, who treasures every word and ponders them in her heart.

It is from this pondering, this reflection, this time of prayer that Mary's wisdom will come. It is from this deepening of her relationship with God that the strength she needs to follow Jesus even to death will be born. It is from the stillness that the courage she needs to approach the empty tomb will grow, developing into the certainty that Christ is risen and the redemption of the human race has begun.

This Christmas I wish you the joy and celebration of the season. I wish you also a time of peace and stillness, enabling you to reflect on everything you see and understand, pondering it in your hearts.

 ## Question

- How are you going to make space to ponder today?

 ## Prayer

May the God of hope fill you with all joy and peace in believing,
so that you may abound in hope by the power of the Holy Spirit.
ROMANS 15:13 (NRSV)

Questions for group study

- Reflecting on this week's Bible passages, which ones have engaged you most? Which have you found most challenging? Has your understanding of love changed and if so, how?

- Think about the many different types of love you have experienced in your lifetime. Share some experiences if you can, or simply name their type. Which have been most satisfying for you, and with which have you struggled most?

❄ Creative prayer

You will need a matchbox and a mirror.

Next time you go for a walk, take a matchbox with you. As you walk, collect beautiful things that catch your eye that will fit in the matchbox. On your return, examine your collection of tiny things. Remember the vision of Julian of Norwich, when she saw a small thing the size of a hazelnut:

> I looked upon it with the eye of my understanding, and thought, 'What may this be?' And it was answered generally thus, 'It is all that is made.' I marvelled how it might last, for I thought it might suddenly have fallen to nothing for littleness. And I was answered in my understanding: 'It lasts and ever shall, for God loves it.' And so have all things their beginning by the love of God. In this little thing I saw three properties. The first is that God made it. The second that God loves it. And the third, that God keeps it.

Look at the things from your matchbox with the eyes of Julian of Norwich. Then look in a mirror, and say out loud: 'God made me. God loves me. God keeps me.'

Week 5 | Monday 26 December–Sunday 1 January

Peace

Beethoven's sixth symphony was completed in 1808 and is one of his most popular works. Drawing upon nature for its inspiration, this pastoral symphony takes us on a walk through the countryside, complete with violent storm in the fourth movement, before ending with a serene sound painting of a rain-washed landscape, colours bright and peace restored. Perhaps peace is not appreciated as much as it should be unless conflict has first been experienced. Perhaps it is simply taken for granted until it is absent.

The intensive study of the concept of peace in the Bible which I have made for the purposes of this book has proved a revelation. Biblical peace is complex and nuanced – it is hard won and often difficult to keep. It is more than a feeling; it is a commitment to a way of life – that way shown to us by the Prince of Peace, whose own life was surrounded by controversy and conflict yet who never broke faith with the principle of peace.

| Monday 26 December

Prophecies

Isaiah 9:6–7

For to us a child is born,
  to us a son is given,
  and the government will be on his shoulders.
And he will be called
  Wonderful Counsellor, Mighty God,
  Everlasting Father, Prince of Peace.
Of the greatness of his government and peace
  there will be no end.
He will reign on David's throne
  and over his kingdom,
establishing and upholding it
  with justice and righteousness
  from that time on and forever.
The zeal of the Lord Almighty
  will accomplish this.

 Reflection

As I write this, there is once again conflict in Israel. Hamas militants and Israeli soldiers are showering rockets upon each other; there is fighting and rioting in the streets of towns and cities and the little town of Bethlehem does not 'lie still'. The situation in the holy city of Jerusalem is full of horror, all of which is brought almost immediately to us by the speed of the internet. We witness daily acts of aggression, see men, women and children torn and bleeding, listen to angry voices shouting at the perceived injustice of the opposite side, and we weep.

Our youngest child, appalled at the sight of a tower block being hit by a rocket and crumbling to the ground, asked me about the origin of the conflict. I could not tell him, as its roots go far back and there is much to be said for the arguments of both sides, each of whom has committed atrocities, each of whom has suffered greatly. Finally I said that Jerusalem was a holy city for three faiths, and faith was something which affected the very heart and soul of people, something for which many would die or kill rather than rescind. The light of the world has been born and the world is still not at peace. The Prince of Peace dwelt among us, and there is still violence and death. The innocent still suffer, and it seems as if the problems will never cease.

Isaiah wrote this passage at a time when the threat of invasion by the neighbouring state of Assyria was becoming a reality. The northern kingdom of Israel was already under the rule of the Assyrian king, Tiglath-Pileser III, and many of Isaiah's prophecies were concerned with the imminent threat to the southern kingdom of Judah. It seems as if the promised land will be torn apart once more, oppressed by invaders, its people exiled and taken into slavery. Over 2,000 years of bitterness and violence, anger and hatred separate us, and still it goes on.

But yet there is hope. For the Messiah, prophesied with so much eagerness and anticipated by Isaiah, has been born. The Son of God has lived with us and shown us in turn how to live. A new kingdom has been established, one of justice and righteousness, where every voice is heard and no one is persecuted. Signs of this 'peaceable kingdom' might at times seem faint and distant, but its echoes surround everyone who strives for peace, working in step with the Prince of Peace, whose reign is steadily gaining hold, despite the best efforts of God's angry, hating, hurting children.

As I pray for poor Jerusalem, I remember a visit I made a few years ago. One evening, at about 8.45 pm, we were in Jerusalem, at the Church of the Holy Sepulchre, which commemorates the site of Jesus' crucifixion, burial and resurrection. Although the church was closing, the crowd did not disperse but waited outside. Clearly something was still to happen, so we waited too.

At 9.00 pm, a man walked out of the church, the door was closed, and he climbed a large stepladder and ceremoniously locked the door. Photos were taken and everyone left. The family of this doorkeeper has held the key to the church for centuries – the oldest document they possess dates to 1517, and the key itself is over 500 years old. More interesting than this, however, is the fact that the family is Muslim. Due to the disputed ownership of the site among Armenian Orthodox, Greek Orthodox, Franciscan and other Christian denominations, a neutral guardian was appointed for the site. Another Muslim family is responsible for opening the site in the morning.

This small gesture of interfaith cooperation shines like a light in the darkness among the disputes, tension and difficulties of Jerusalem and the surrounding countryside. We witnessed other 'lights' also – signs of hope not just to the country's inhabitants but to all who seek to bring peace from conflict. And so I join my prayers with others all over the world as we continue to pray for peace in the Middle East, believing with Isaiah that 'of the greatness of [God's] government and of peace there will be no end'.

 Questions

- How might you work for peace in your community?

- Are there areas in your life which are torn by conflict – unhappy relationships, quarrels with neighbours? Is there a way in which peaceable solutions can be found?

Prayer

Lord,
lead us from death to life,
from falsehood to truth.
Lead us from despair to hope,
from fear to trust.
Let peace fill our hearts, our world and our universe.
Let us dream together, pray together and work together,
to build one world of peace and justice for all.

Author unknown – it is thought to be an adaptation either of a Hindu prayer or of a hymn. The first time that it was known to be publicly spoken was by Mother Teresa in 1981.

| Tuesday 27 December

Journeys

Revelation 1:4–6 (ISV)

> From John to the seven churches in Asia. May grace and peace be yours from the one who is, who was, and who is coming, from the seven spirits who are in front of his throne, and from Jesus the Messiah, the witness, the faithful one, the firstborn from the dead, and the ruler over the kings of the earth. To the one who loves us and has freed us from our sins by his blood and has made us a kingdom, priests for his God and Father, be glory and power forever and ever! Amen.

 ## Reflection

What a beautiful way to begin a letter – sending grace and peace. The words John uses are even more loaded with meaning.

Charis, or grace, is also used to describe the Roman system of patronage, by which the patron supported and encouraged individuals and groups and received loyalty and service from them in return. Vestiges of this system remain in the art and music world, where wealthy individuals or companies support artists or even entire orchestras, obtaining prime seats at events as well as the associated kudos in return. So perhaps John is describing a relationship whereby we gain a sense of belonging from being a Christian, supported and encouraged in our life journey as we offer Christ our loyalty and service in recognition of the gift that has been bestowed upon us, unworthy as we are.

To contemporary readers, this doesn't sound particularly challenging, until we put it in the context in which John was writing, when patrons had great control over those who served them and expected much in the way of obligation in return for any favour shown. To have Christ as a patron meant loyalty to God came first above everything else, obligation to ones fellow Christians being more important than obligation to those who held earthly power.

In the same way, the use of the word *eirene* for peace calls to mind the Pax Romana, that period of stability, prosperity and order which lasted for some hundreds of years of Roman imperial rule. This 'peace' was enforced through the might and power of the emperors, from Caesar Augustus to Marcus Aurelius. But once again, John is challenging the status quo – if peace comes from God and not the Roman emperor, who holds the real power?

This is reinforced by John in verse 5 as he lists out the attributes of Jesus, including 'ruler over the kings of the earth'. By sending us grace and peace, God undermines the earthly system of power, reminding all Christians where their loyalties lie and upon whom their eyes should be fixed. Our God, John reminds us, has more power than the mightiest emperor, offers more support than the most powerful of patrons, and rules over the rulers.

It is this God who loves us, forgives us and offers us a place in his kingdom. It is this God who has existed since before the beginning of time and will reign long after time itself has ceased to exist. It is this God whose message is carried by John. Into the midst of the persecution, torture and destruction of Christians which was being carried out at the time this letter was written comes this clarion call of hope and faith. This is the peace that is being offered to us – a peace which is everlasting and indestructible, strong and true.

Surrounded by the aftermath of Christmas, we might be tempted to look ahead with anxious anticipation to the dark months of winter. Some of us will be facing challenging times and there will be few of us who do not long for the approach of spring. John's greeting reminds us of our membership of a vast community of saints, stretching behind and before us, encouraging us to have faith in the bringer of grace and peace, whose rule extends over all and whose kingdom is, and was, and is coming.

 ## Questions

- Spend some time examining your loyalties. Where do they lie? Which communities are important to you and why? Should they have the influence over you that they do?

- How can you send grace and peace to someone else today?

 ## Prayer

All hail the power of Jesus' name!
Let angels prostrate fall.
Bring forth the royal diadem,
and crown him Lord of all.

Edward Perronet (1726–92)

Babies

Isaiah 11:6–10

The wolf will live with the lamb,
    the leopard will lie down with the goat,
the calf and the lion and the yearling together;
    and a little child will lead them.
The cow will feed with the bear,
    their young will lie down together,
    and the lion will eat straw like the ox.
The infant will play near the cobra's den,
    and the young child will put its hand into the viper's nest.
They will neither harm nor destroy
    on all my holy mountain,
for the earth will be filled with the knowledge of the Lord
    as the waters cover the sea.
In that day the Root of Jesse will stand as a banner for the peoples; the nations will rally to him, and his resting-place will be glorious.

 Reflection

I have been very fortunate to have spent much of my life surrounded by babies and young children. Time spent with younger siblings, then my own four children, followed closely by grandchildren, has been swelled by time spent leading toddler groups, crèches, family services and Messy Church – all gloriously noisy, chaotic, joyful and interesting as I have watched each generation grow and become independent, caring for others just as they were cared for in their turn.

That is another constant – the fragility of small people, their helplessness, their tendency to get into danger, their dependence on others for their survival. When Isaiah wrote this passage, historians estimate that the mortality rate for young children was one in four – that is, every fourth newborn died in the first year of life, and one out of two died in childhood, according to **ourworldindata.org/child-mortality**. People have assumed that because of this, the attachment of parents to their young children was less than it is nowadays. Surely, they reason, if there is only a 50 per cent chance of your child surviving, you detach yourself from it, save yourself from the pain of bereavement. I am not so sure. Who, having carried a child in their body for nine months, brought it to birth and cared for it, could then distance themselves? I am guessing that the pain of watching your baby fall sick and die in Roman times was every bit as hard as it is today.

This statistic means that almost every household would have experienced infant death and would be familiar with the pain of losing someone for whom they were responsible, perhaps suffering the guilt of feeling they should have been able to protect them. Isaiah's prophecy would have sparked the imagination of the reader or listener, encouraging visions of a time when all these precious lives would be saved, when threat of danger or disease would be taken away and a long-lived future would be available for everyone.

But we are not there yet. The infant Christ has arrived in our world. Already his life is in danger, as Herod plots his slaughter. Soon he will become a refugee, one of the most fragile states of existence there is. Once he has survived that, he will experience the usual illnesses and accidents of childhood. How odd that God chose to place the means of redemption for all humankind in so frail a vessel! But it is in sharing our griefs as well as our joys that Christ journeys alongside us, encouraging and loving us as we encounter everything that life throws at us. The peace Isaiah describes is that of all creatures living harmoniously together, no longer having to compete for resources, but able to share the plenty that is available in ways that benefit everyone. The peace that Christ brings is of a world committed to sharing, with nations gathering as one to defeat the common enemies of disease and disaster.

We still have a long way to go before that peace is a reality. Although infant mortality rates have fallen everywhere, there are still countries, in sub-Saharan Africa, for example, where the rate is greater than ten per cent. One in ten children born today will not live beyond their fifth birthday. That is 15,000 young children every day whose lives will be cut short, whose parents, siblings and relations will be stricken with grief, whose communities will suffer the loss of so much unfulfilled potential. Those of us in more privileged countries might feel helpless in the face of such statistics, but there will always be ways of making a difference. It is up to each one of us to contribute in any way we can to promote the well-being of infants and children, in our own community and across the globe.

Question

- What single thing can you do today to advance the well-being of infants and children, whether in your own family, neighbourhood or further afield?

Benediction

In these days, God says, I will pour out my Spirit upon all people.

May God's Spirit anoint your dreams and visions, for you are painters of peace.

May God's Spirit anoint your murmurs and your songs, for you are heralds of justice.

May God's Spirit anoint your youngest and oldest, for you are communities of change.

In your rising, in your resting, in your walking, in your speaking, in your praying, in your striving, in your giving, in your crying, may you know the Spirit of the Lord upon you.

May she labour through you and in you, and all those who stand with you, until that day when freedom resounds throughout God's earth, and justice rolls down, and righteousness streams out, and all God's children know that blessing that belongs to us all.

Christian Aid

| Thursday 29 December

Signs

Matthew 2:16–18

When Herod realised that he had been outwitted by the Magi, he was furious, and he gave orders to kill all the boys in Bethlehem and its vicinity who were two years old and under, in accordance with the time he had learned from the Magi. Then what was said through the prophet Jeremiah was fulfilled:

'A voice is heard in Ramah,
weeping and great mourning,
Rachel weeping for her children
and refusing to be comforted,
because they are no more.'

 Reflection

I recently spoke at a webinar designed to give schools and churches some information on pilgrimage spirituality and some suggestions as to how their communities might explore the idea of pilgrimage. One of my fellow speakers spoke very movingly about a pilgrimage he had made with his younger daughter from his home town to Canterbury Cathedral. On the way they stopped at the café where he had first asked out the young woman who was to become his wife and the mother of his children. 'It then all got a bit existential,' he continued, 'because I said to my daughter, "If I hadn't asked her out, you wouldn't be here."' An interesting concept to discuss with a young person – 'What if?'

Holy Innocents Day comes crashing into the festivities of Christmas with as much sensitivity as a tank at a wedding. The air still echoes with our tender injunctions to the infant Christ to 'sleep in heavenly peace', we are riding high on a wave of 'peace on earth and goodwill to all people', and then Herod's obscene commands pierce the tranquillity, and instead of choirs of angels we hear Rachel mourning for her children 'and refusing to be comforted'.

More than anything, this passage highlights the gap between the 'now' and the 'not yet', between God's promises for us and our all too human resistance to them, as seen in Herod's stubborn adherence to his wicked and selfish ways, taking desperate measures to cling on to whatever power he has gained, frightened at the threat that a mere infant can bring to his rule.

'How could God have allowed such suffering?', we might well cry out, weeping in horror at the cruelty shown with such abandonment to the most vulnerable members of the community. God did not cause the suffering, we are reminded; Herod did, in his greed, fear and anger. God does not meet anger with violence, slaughter with hatred. Instead, God embraces this most difficult of all stories by sending his Son to inhabit a world which can allow such cruelty – to inhabit, to challenge and finally to transform by a supreme and final act of love. The events of the first few months of Jesus' life demonstrate to us that there is no area of human experience that he is not willing to enter, no danger that he will not face with us, no situation which is beyond reach of his healing.

What if? What if Herod had succeeded in his plan? What if Joseph had not heeded the dream the angel sent him? What would be the hope for our world then? What if we forget, in times of pain, distress or sadness, that the king of love is with us at all times? What if we allow our greed and selfishness to crowd out the opportunities we are given for generosity and love? What if we stop believing in the Prince of Peace, but allow the wickedness of human nature to overwhelm us?

Holy Innocents Day reminds us to stand by the innocent victims of war, injustice, disaster – all the things which daily overwhelm our fellow human beings. It reminds us that while the birth of Christ brings the victory of good over evil, the battle is not yet done. Above all, it reminds us that because of Christ's birth and death, those who mourn will, in the end, be comforted.

Question

- Wonder at some of the events in your life. What if they had not happened? Wonder at the goodness which has been shown to you.

Prayer

Heavenly Father,
whose children suffered at the hands of Herod,
though they had done no wrong:
by the suffering of your Son
and by the innocence of our lives,
frustrate all evil designs
and establish your reign of justice and peace;
through Jesus Christ your Son our Lord,
who is alive and reigns with you,
in the unity of the Holy Spirit,
one God, now and forever.
Amen

Friday 30 December

Poems

Psalm 85:8–11

> I will listen to what God the Lord says;
>   he promises peace to his people, his faithful servants –
>   but let them not turn to folly.
> Surely his salvation is near those who fear him,
>   that his glory may dwell in our land.
> Love and faithfulness meet together;
>   righteousness and peace kiss each other.
> Faithfulness springs forth from the earth,
>   and righteousness looks down from heaven.

 Reflection

One of the regular features of the family service in a church I used to attend was the final song, 'Shalom My Friend'. A congregational favourite, it was made more poignant by the practice of every church member circulating and shaking hands with others as they sang. The singing became a bit wobbly as the handshakes grew more enthusiastic, and occasionally conversations sprang up while the hymn was still in play, but nonetheless the activity was moving and powerful. Different generations of worshippers would wish each other 'Shalom' and hope to meet again in a way which summarised for me the open-hearted and welcoming nature of the church community. Families and friends, strangers old and young, would all offer friendship and support, mutual acknowledgement of belonging, to the benefit of the entire community.

These verses from Psalm 85 help to spell out the nature of 'shalom', the peace which was being offered by each church member to whoever was willing to accept it. Shalom is promised to those who keep faith with God, who do not fall prey to the countless distractions of the secular world, whether these are the glittering delights of power and wealth or the darker temptations of cynicism and despair. All these types of 'folly' lure Christians away from the path of hope and faith, beguiling us with false promises of an easier way or enticing us into the 'slough of despond' made famous by John Bunyan in his allegorical *The Pilgrim's Progress*. That is not to say that shalom is denied to those whose suffering, whether spiritual, mental or physical, is genuine. For those troubled ones the hope of salvation is extended, made certain through the death and resurrection of Christ, whose own suffering redeems and transforms ours.

Just as the sight of young children and elderly men and women shaking hands offers a glimpse of God's kingdom to those who have the eyes of faith to perceive it, so Psalm 85 shares a glimpse of the components of shalom. True, lasting peace is found wherever 'love and faithfulness' are to be found – wherever brave souls continue to love despite persecution or rejection, wherever faith shines through apathy and secularism. Peace surrounds those who work for peace with righteousness, not content with a peace which is merely the absence of war, but striving instead for that deep peace which springs from every individual being valued, honoured and accepted, their contribution to society treated with respect, however much or little they are able to bring.

Shalom for most of us – individuals, communities, nations – is still just a hope, a vision, a hint of what is to come. But we can still catch a glimpse of it, experience its fulfilment for a moment – perhaps when we join with our community in worship; perhaps when we witness one of those everyday miracles of nature which are given so abundantly to us in sunsets, flowers, clouds or young animals; or perhaps when we hear the voice of one we love or simply hear a child laugh.

Questions

- When have you known 'shalom'? How do you make the most of those moments?

 ## Prayer

Heavenly Father, thank you for the glimpses of your peace that we witness in our lives. We pray for a time when the glimpse becomes a full experience, when your righteousness is fulfilled on earth as it now looks down from heaven. Amen

Stories

Acts 9:31 (NRSV)

Meanwhile the church throughout Judea, Galilee, and Samaria had peace and was built up. Living in the fear of the Lord and in the comfort of the Holy Spirit, it increased in numbers.

 ## Reflection

'What are you writing about at the moment?' asked an interested colleague.

'That part in Acts about how the church had peace and was built up and increased in numbers,' I replied.

'Huh,' pronounced my colleague. 'A church at peace? I would like to see that one!'

To be fair, the person I was talking to was in a particularly heated dispute around the disposition of church furniture, so was feeling rather jaded at the time. Many months spent wrangling not only with one's own community but with various interested heritage bodies had left them exhausted and cynical. However, I felt I could sympathise with their viewpoint, and I am sure that is the same for many people.

How many of us have experienced churches in conflict, whether that conflict is caused by worship styles, choice of leaders, strategies for mission or simply the removal or otherwise of pews from the building?

And these are just the conflicts which are engaged in by the whole community – never mind the various personal disagreements or fallings out, arguments and hurt feelings of individuals and groups. In my experience this was exacerbated during the months when church buildings were closed because of Covid-19. We were unable to meet and chat, exchange quick greetings, sort out small misunderstandings before they became major issues, or remind ourselves how fond we really were of our fellow Christians, despite their annoying habits and actions. When finally allowed back into the building once more, the air could be cleared and miscommunications put right, enabling us to rejoice in the privilege of gathering together to pray.

'Peace' is hard work. There is an expectation that peace just happens, that provided everyone is careful of everyone else's feelings the result will be an easy, settled, peaceful community. But the longer I am alive, the more certain I become that real peace – solid, lasting peace – is built with effort, patience, tolerance and understanding. Brick by careful brick, a foundation of principles is created – the way we speak to each other; the way we listen; the way we collaborate; the way we include each other and work together; and, above all, the way we forgive, time after time, offence after insult, admitting our errors just as we set aside the errors of others, allowing God's grace to work within each one of us as we do his work.

It is worth noting that this passage in Acts comes directly after the story of Paul's conversion on the road to Damascus. Although Paul preaches so powerfully in Damascus that he has to escape in a basket to avoid the anger of the Jews, he is met with a different reaction on his arrival in Jerusalem. There, his reputation as Saul the Christian-slayer means that although he tries to join the disciples, they are afraid of him. It is not until Barnabas witnesses to Paul's actions in Damascus that Paul is allowed to go 'in and out among them… speaking boldly in the name of the Lord' (Acts 9:28). Even in the early church there is disagreement and fear. Trust must be won and communities must be encouraged and cared for; only then can peace grow and spread.

The story of the early church demonstrates the importance of learning to live together, working to overcome disagreements, communicating carefully and sensitively, offering to God the worship which is his due and prioritising the work of the kingdom. These things are all aspects of 'living in the fear of the Lord and in the comfort of the Holy Spirit'. They spring from peace and produce peace in their turn, and so vibrant and loving is the community which develops that people cannot help but be drawn to it. This is our ambition for our own church communities – that what we demonstrate in the way we live is so attractive that others will wish to hear the gospel we so wish to share.

 ## Questions

- How would you define a 'peaceful church'? What could your church do to become more 'peace-filled'?

 ## Prayer

Loving God, give to our church the willingness to work for peace. Encourage us as we listen and love, share and forgive, so that we might truly reflect your purposes for our community. Amen

| Sunday 1 January

Conversations – with Christ

John 20:19–23

> On the evening of that first day of the week, when the disciples were together, with the doors locked for fear of the Jewish leaders, Jesus came and stood among them and said, 'Peace be with you!' After he said this, he showed them his hands and side. The disciples were overjoyed when they saw the Lord.
>
> Again Jesus said, 'Peace be with you! As the Father has sent me, I am sending you.' And with that he breathed on them and said, 'Receive the Holy Spirit. If you forgive anyone's sins, their sins are forgiven; if you do not forgive them, they are not forgiven.'

 ## Reflection

What a wonderful gift for the beginning of the year – how precious to be starting 2023 with the peace of Christ! During the last week we have grieved for the places in the world still torn apart by conflict, mourned with innocent victims and explored the challenge of peace in difficult circumstances. We have discerned that while true peace can always be found, it can also be fleeting, offering only glimpses of the reality which lies behind all things. And we have reflected on the difficulty of making and keeping peace in our communities. Yet here is Jesus himself, offering us peace, freely and without condition.

The reality of Jesus' death is just sinking in for the d
things have been complicated by Mary Magdalene's asse
has 'seen the Lord' (John 20:18). I suspect that few of the disciples
believed her – after all, it is a truly incredible statement she is making.
Perhaps when she told them the story of her encounter with the risen
Christ she mentioned that she first thought he was the gardener, and
perhaps secretly many of them still thought he was. But there they
are, on the first day of the week, gathered together as they always
have in the past. Because where else is there to go, what else is there
to do except repeat the activities of the past three glorious, enriching,
prayer-filled years of following Jesus, hearing his stories, witnessing
his miracles, learning about God's kingdom?

And suddenly there he is, in their midst. And how does he announce
his arrival? By bringing peace. This is the peace of God, offered to us
all, undeserving as we are. By its grace we are enabled to live our
lives without worry, confident that although we might not know what
the future holds, we can be sure God holds the future. We can work
for peace, knowing that this is vital kingdom work and that, however
small our contribution, it will be taken and multiplied, added to the
offerings of millions of others as the Prince of Peace expands his reign.

Two further things are offered at this first meeting – the Holy Spirit
and the injunction to forgive. Filled with the Holy Spirit, again given
freely and unconditionally, our response can only be to forgive those
who have caused us hurt, wipe the slate clean so that we and they
can begin again.

As the new year lies before us, with all its potential, let us put behind
us those memories which fester and poison us as we hold on to old
grudges and bitterness. Let us ask the Holy Spirit to wash us clean so
that we might begin the new year with 'clean hearts and minds', ready
to do God's work wherever it is asked of us, rejoicing in the gift of his
peace and offering that gift to others in turn.

Questions

- Who might you need to forgive today? From whom should you ask for forgiveness?

 ## Prayer

When peace like a river attendeth my way,
when sorrows like sea billows roll;
whatever my lot, thou hast taught me to say,
'It is well, it is well with my soul.'

Horatio Gates Spafford (1828–88)

Questions for group study

- Reflecting on this week's Bible passages, which ones have engaged you most? Which have you found most challenging? Has your understanding of peace changed and if so, how?

- Where do you find your peace?

- How might your community become part of the peaceable kingdom?

Creative prayer

You will need a square of paper.

Sadako Sasaki was a Japanese girl who was living in Hiroshima when the atomic bomb was dropped on the city at the end of World War II. Stricken with leukemia, she struggled to make paper cranes, following the legend that if someone made 1,000 they would be granted a wish.

The idea caught the imagination of children everywhere and in 1958 a life-size statue of a crane was erected in Hiroshima's Peace Park bearing the legend, 'This is our cry, this is our prayer, peace in the world.'

We don't need to make 1,000, but you could make at least one, praying for peace as you do.

Instructions for making a paper crane can be found at **wikihow.com/Fold-a-Paper-Crane** or in any good origami book.

Week 6 | Monday 2 January–Friday 6 January

Hope

One of my favourite pictures is an engraving by Edward Burne-Jones. Entitled 'Hope', it is a study for bigger, more complicated depictions of Hope. It is engraved in gold and shows a figure emerging from a stone tomb into a barren landscape. The figure has her arms uplifted – there is grace and supplication in the gesture. She is escaping death but her new environment does not look much more welcoming. And yet, there is such movement in the picture, such energy, that we cannot help but be filled with hope for what will become.

As we enter the new year, let us do so with the energy of hope. And let us look to the God of grace to support us as we journey on.

Prophecies

Isaiah 61:8–10a (NRSV)

For I the Lord love justice,
    I hate robbery and wrongdoing;
I will faithfully give them their recompense,
    and I will make an everlasting covenant with them.
Their descendants shall be known among the nations,
    and their offspring among the peoples;
all who see them shall acknowledge
    that they are a people whom the Lord has blessed.
I will greatly rejoice in the Lord,
    my whole being shall exult in my God;
for he has clothed me with the garments of salvation.

 Reflection

We are back in Isaiah again – that prophecy of hope, written when things seemed at their darkest for the children of Israel. This time the prophet is not encouraging a people in exile, but a people returned and disappointed. Everything they had hoped and planned for seems to be going wrong. The temple is not being rebuilt as quickly as everyone had hoped and the city turning out not to be as glorious as planned. Some of the same old mistakes are being made, and shoddy, ill-thought-out construction is taking place.

Worse still, a people who suffered so greatly after their forced exile are somehow not responding as well as they could now that they are back in their homeland. The expectation was that once the pain and suffering of exile was removed, people would respond with joy and thanksgiving – their behaviour would be honest and just, and the old issues of corruption, dissent and in-fighting among different factions would cease. But human beings are who they are; the challenges of living together have not been surmounted, and it seems as if everything is as it was.

How does Isaiah teach them to behave amid this disappointment and apathy? To rejoice! To put on the 'garments of salvation', to celebrate. If we live in hope, believing that a better, fairer future is ours for the living, then we are more likely to work to make that reality come about. If we determine to rejoice in our salvation, our status as children of God, then we are more likely to live as people of the kingdom.

There is an often-quoted expression by Mahatma Gandhi – 'Be the change you want to see in the world.' As with so many famous 'quotes', Gandhi didn't actually say these words – they are a precis of a longer discourse:

> We but mirror the world. All the tendencies present in the outer world are to be found in the world of our body. If we could change ourselves, the tendencies in the world would also change. As a man changes his own nature, so does the attitude of the world change towards him. This is the divine mystery supreme. A wonderful thing it is and the source of our happiness. We need not wait to see what others do.
>
> *The Collected Works of Mahatma Gandhi*, vol. 12 (Ministry of Information and Broadcasting, 1964)

This quote actually mirrors Isaiah's instructions more closely than the shortened version, with its idea that our attitude to the world affects how the world treats us. This is a commonplace, but is worth repeating and reinforcing since, as with so much commonly received wisdom, it is often paid lip service but less often enacted. The follow-on to this is also that the world itself will change as more people act with righteousness and justice towards others, spreading like ripples from a stone in a pool, which disturb the surface of current behaviour and attitudes, encouraging change and growth.

So let us not 'wait and see what others do'. Let us take heart from the promises of God and work with hope for a better, freer, more peaceful world.

 ## Questions

- What is the difference between the attributed quote and Gandhi's actual words? Which do you think is the more powerful?

 ## Prayer

Lord God, help me to be an instrument for change. Help me to disturb and disrupt current ways of thinking that are unjust and apathetic. Help me to live as if my hopes for the world can be achieved, and to rejoice accordingly. Amen

| Tuesday 3 January

Journeys

John 14:1–7 (NRSV)

'Do not let your hearts be troubled. Believe in God, believe also in me. In my Father's house there are many dwelling-places. If it were not so, would I have told you that I go to prepare a place for you? And if I go and prepare a place for you, I will come again and will take you to myself, so that where I am, there you may be also. And you know the way to the place where I am going.' Thomas said to him, 'Lord, we do not know where you are going. How can we know the way?' Jesus said to him, 'I am the way, and the truth, and the life. No one comes to the Father except through me. If you know me, you will know my Father also. From now on you do know him and have seen him.'

 ## Reflection

I love this passage. I love the sheer humanity that it reflects and the hope that it brings for all of us. This is one of Jesus' final conversations with his disciples before his death. He knows the path he must take in a short while. He feels anxiety and love for those he is leaving behind and is hastening to cram in a final few instructions before his departure – to give them something to hang on to after he has gone. So he offers reassurance and comfort – it's okay, don't be afraid; I am not going away forever; I am only going ahead of you and that's not so bad because after all, you know the way.

Only they don't. Three years this group of men have walked with Jesus. They have witnessed countless healings, heard his stories. They have eaten with him and prayed with him. They have been accepted by towns and turned away from them. And still they misunderstand! How incredible is that – and yet how reassuring.

The lack of comprehension of the disciples – their failure to grasp what Jesus is about, and their inability to believe truly that he is the Son of God, the Messiah and to inhabit that belief – all this gives us space to doubt. How can we, who have not had the privilege of journeying with Jesus, possibly understand what they could not? No wonder we struggle at times! No wonder we lack faith when we are assailed by misfortune, conflicted with doubt, challenged when God fails to answer our prayers. Even the disciples felt the same. We can take comfort from that, and find the answer in Jesus' response to his beloved friends and companions: 'I am the way.' Simple. If you know Jesus, you will know God. If you walk in Jesus' ways, you will encounter the King of Kings.

And what are Jesus' ways? It would seem at first as if they are restrictive – Jesus only gives us one way, one truth, one life. In the past, and even in places today, this phrase has been used to corral entire congregations into a single way of acting. It has been used to force people whose behaviour is not considered 'acceptable' to conform to rigid codes. It has been used as an excuse for all sorts of inhospitable behaviour, all sorts of discrimination and many acts of hatred and injustice. What a tragic misreading of the way.

Jesus' way is full of love and light. Jesus' way is one where a farmer scatters seeds everywhere, not just in the places where they have traditionally grown, but joyfully, liberally, everywhere, in the hope that some of these seeds will sprout and multiply and fill the kingdom. Jesus' way is one where outcasts are valued, children are welcome, and the poor and the sick are healed. Jesus' way is one that allows business to break off to pay attention to a woman who touches his robe, that ignores prejudice and has tea with a tax collector, and that honours the copper of a widow's donation as much as the gold of a ruler's. Jesus' way, in short, is broad and inclusive, welcoming and nurturing, thoughtful and respectful.

And if we walk in Jesus' way, we will find it leads to the Father.

 # Questions

- What are your ideas on heaven? Does this image of a house with 'many mansions' (KJV) help?

- How might you follow Jesus' way more closely today?

 # Prayer

Lord, give me grace to tread in thy steps and conform me to thy divine image, that the more I grow like thee, the more I may love thee, and the more I may be loved by thee.

Bishop Thomas Ken (1637–1711)

Babies

Isaiah 65:17–21

'See, I will create
    new heavens and a new earth.
The former things will not be remembered,
    nor will they come to mind.
But be glad and rejoice forever
    in what I will create,
for I will create Jerusalem to be a delight
    and its people a joy.
I will rejoice over Jerusalem
    and take delight in my people;
the sound of weeping and of crying
    will be heard in it no more.
Never again will there be in it
    an infant who lives but a few days,
    or an old man who does not live out his years;
the one who dies at a hundred
    will be thought a mere child;
the one who fails to reach a hundred
    will be considered accursed.
They will build houses and dwell in them;
    they will plant vineyards and eat their fruit.'

 Reflection

The baptism of a child is a wonderful event. Whether it takes place as part of the regular Sunday service or if only the family and friends are gathered together, the atmosphere is joyful and relaxed. If there are lots of young children present, the inevitable chaos only adds to the sense of celebration. I spend time with the parents beforehand, running through the service so that we all know more or less what we will be doing and talking to them about the gift of the Holy Spirit which will be given at baptism.

I rejoice in the theology of the efficacy of the Holy Spirit, who does not rely on the willingness or understanding of the recipient to work. I celebrate the fact that baptism is once for always – the outward signing of the cross and bathing in water can never be undone or repeated but remains a permanent feature, imprinted on a person's soul. I marvel at the profundity and depth of the sacrament and never underestimate the seriousness of the event, however anarchic the service itself might seem to be.

And undergirding it all is a deep sense of hope. The parents are filled with hope for the child's future in all its aspects. We pray that the child will grow up secure and happy, that they will be able to lead fulfilling and purposeful lives. We acknowledge that difficult and challenging times are part of the lot of human beings, and we pray that the child will have access to inner resources and external support to overcome such times and continue to thrive and grow. We hope that the child learns how to walk with God, that they access the blessings which are given to them with the gift of the Spirit and that they find a home within a Christian community.

The blessings which we pray for every child find a source in this passage in Isaiah, where we are reminded once more of the promises of God for each one of us. Echoed by John in Revelation, we are promised a 'new heaven and a new earth'. We are encouraged to look forward in faith to a time when 'there will be no more weeping and crying' (Revelation 21:4). We live in hope that babies will not die before their time, that old men and women will live in peace to their allotted end. We trust that we will find in death not an ending but a new beginning as the journey continues on a different plane.

Hope for a world where all can live in harmony and peace, where everyone will be able to 'plant vineyards and eat their fruit', should not be looked upon as foolish or irresponsibly optimistic. Hope is part of our life's blood – through it we find meaning and purpose for all that we do, as we work for better times, with a vision for a future in which the will of God is fulfilled and the new kingdom brought into being.

 ## Question

- What are your hopes for the future?

 ## Prayer

Then he said to me, 'It is done! I am the Alpha and the Omega, the beginning and the end. To the thirsty I will give water as a gift from the spring of the water of life. Those who conquer will inherit these things, and I will be their God and they will be my children.
REVELATION 21:6–7 (NRSV)

Signs

Luke 2:36–38

> There was also a prophet, Anna, the daughter of Penuel, of the tribe of Asher. She was very old; she had lived with her husband seven years after her marriage, and then was a widow until she was eighty-four. She never left the temple but worshipped night and day, fasting and praying. Coming up to them at that very moment, she gave thanks to God and spoke about the child to all who were looking forward to the redemption of Jerusalem.

 Reflection

In my pilgrim journeys I have had the privilege of walking alongside many different people, of all ages and background. One of the most interesting groups is comprised of those who have recently retired. Many of these are carrying out a promise made to themselves over many years – that they would celebrate the end of their period of full-time paid employment by making a significant journey. Others have only taken on board the idea of a pilgrimage in the few months preceding their retirement. And a few have set off on the spur of a moment, with little planning, simply heading out towards a distant destination.

Conversations with these fellow pilgrims have been interesting, surprising and occasionally very moving. Many walkers embrace the time for reflection, giving themselves space to look back over everything they have been and done and to give thanks for it. Some are looking forward to the next stage of their lives, using the rhythm of walking as a background for thinking about their priorities and goals for the future. They have shared the experience and wisdom of years, as well as their hopes for the years ahead, and I have been the richer for it.

The story of Anna is one of wisdom and hope. There is always a danger of disregarding the contribution that those who are no longer in financially rewarding work can bring to society as a whole, and it is wonderful to read how Anna's faithfulness and prayer is rewarded by her glimpse of the Messiah. Her willingness to share her experience is also documented – she speaks about Jesus as one who will be instrumental in the 'redemption of Jerusalem'. Anna has not stopped looking forward, and she has not ceased to live in hope. Her story honours her in its inclusion in the narration of Jesus birth.

How appropriate, therefore, that the work of BRF in supporting the elderly should be called Anna Chaplaincy in her honour. Anna Chaplains work within communities to accompany older people at this age and stage of their lives. Complementing existing ministry, it offers spiritual care by helping people reflect on their life's journey – both the joys and the sorrows – and, where appropriate, enabling the healing of memories and the celebration of life experiences to foster more hope and resilience. It recognises the contribution older people can make to society, but also speaks out in their support, championing their needs and acting on their behalf within a wider context. Part of a wider team resourced and licensed by BRF, Anna Chaplains make a real difference in the communities in which they work – a brave and exciting venture.

Each of us, whatever our age and abilities, can contribute to the wellbeing of society, not just in active ways, but, like Anna herself, by being a model of prayer and faithfulness. We can look to the future with hope, articulating our vision for a better world, enthusing and supporting others in their work as the body of Christ carries out God's work on earth.

Questions

- Are the needs and contributions of older people recognised in your community? How could that be improved?

 ## Prayer

On the contrary, the members of the body that seem to be weaker are indispensable, and those members of the body that we think less honourable we clothe with greater honour, and our less respectable members are treated with greater respect; whereas our more respectable members do not need this. But God has so arranged the body, giving the greater honour to the inferior member, that there may be no dissension within the body, but the members may have the same care for one another.

1 CORINTHIANS 12:22–25 (NRSV)

| Friday 6 January

Stories

Matthew 2:10–12 (NRSV)

When they saw that the star had stopped, they were overwhelmed with joy. On entering the house, they saw the child with Mary his mother; and they knelt down and paid him homage. Then, opening their treasure chests, they offered him gifts of gold, frankincense and myrrh. And having been warned in a dream not to return to Herod, they left for their own country by another road.

 Reflection

And so, with the arrival of the wise men at the end of their journey, we arrive at the end of our journey through Advent and beyond. But just like the wise men, our journey does not end here. They had to travel back to their own countries, carrying with them tales of their journey and memories of the new Messiah, the hope of the world. We travel on, treasuring all that we have learnt and reflected upon, the insights we have gained and the prayers we have spoken.

We take with us something of the wisdom of those travellers from long ago as well.

We can be prepared, like them, to leave our comfort zones and step out boldly in faith, following the guidance of the Spirit and trusting to God that he will lead us in the right paths, so that we may truly fulfil the purposes he has for us.

We can seek the truth, not leaving the task to others, but prepared to join in the work of the kingdom, willingly accepting the risks and to engage personally in the work of faith.

We can ask for help along the way, learning from those who have gone before us, accepting offers of help and support, resourcing others in our turn.

And finally, we can rejoice in the evidence of God's love which surrounds us, looking for signs of the kingdom and celebrating them when we find them.

Thank you for journeying with me this far. I pray for you as you travel on.

 Prayer

May the road rise up to meet you.
May the wind be always at your back.
May the sun shine warm upon your face;
the rains fall soft upon your fields
and until we meet again,
may God hold you in the palm of his hand.
Anonymous Celtic blessing

Some final reflections

- What have I learned about myself during this period?

- What have I learned about God?

- How might I sustain a practice of prayer and reflection?

- How might I share all that God means to me – and all that he could mean to others?

 ## Creative prayer

You will need children's bubble mixture, or a 1:1 solution of washing-up liquid and water, and a piece of wire bent into a circle with a handle for holding.

Blow some prayer bubbles. As you watch the bubbles float up into the air, pray for hope for all those who are troubled in mind, body or spirit. Pray that the Spirit of God may be breathed into them, so that they might find peace. Pray for yourself, that you will be lifted up before the Lord, to rejoice in his love.

Sustaining your daily journey
with the Bible

New Daylight is ideal for anyone wanting an accessible yet stimulating aid to spending time with God each day, deepening their faith and their knowledge of scripture. Each issue provides four months of daily Bible readings and comment, with a team of regular contributors drawn from a range of church backgrounds and covering a varied selection of Old and New Testament, biblical themes, characters and seasonal readings. Each daily section includes a short Bible passage (text included), thought-provoking comment and a prayer or point for reflection.

New Daylight is edited by Gordon Giles and is published three times a year in January, May and September. Available in regular and deluxe editions with large print, as a daily email and as an app for Android, iPhone and iPad.

brfonline.org.uk

Using the metaphor of pilgrimage, Sally Welch walks alongside us as leader and guide, but also fellow traveller, to explore how we can understand this biblical principle and make it our own. This book is divided into sections of a journey, beginning with the preparations necessary before setting out, exploring the obstacles which might be put in our path and sharing ways in which the journey can be made easier and more productive. At the end of each reflection there is a suggestion for an activity or prayer to enable the reader to apply the learning to their own life.

Journey to Contentment
Pilgrimage principles for everyday life
Sally Welch
978 0 85746 592 4 £8.99

brfonline.org.uk

Why do pilgrims walk so much? What do they learn? What lasting good does it do? Experienced pilgrim and writer Sally Welch explores the less-travelled pilgrim routes of the UK and beyond, through the eyes of the pilgrims who walk them. Each chapter explores a different aspect of pilgrimage, offering reflections and indicating some of the spiritual lessons to be learned that may be practised at home. This absorbing book shows how insights gained on the journey can be incorporated into the spiritual life of every day, bringing new ways of relationship with God and with our fellow Christians.

Pilgrim Journeys
Pilgrimage for walkers and armchair travellers
Sally Welch
978 0 85746 513 9 £7.99

brfonline.org.uk

Enabling all ages to grow in faith

Anna Chaplaincy
Living Faith
Messy Church
Parenting for Faith

100 years of BRF

2022 is BRF's 100th anniversary! Look out for details of our special new centenary resources, a beautiful centenary rose and an online thanksgiving service that we hope you'll attend. This centenary year we're focusing on sharing the story of BRF, the story of the Bible – and we hope you'll share your stories of faith with us too.

Find out more at **brf.org.uk/centenary**.

To find out more about our work, visit
brf.org.uk

Sharing
the Story
since 1922